R. Mukund has over 40 y[...] production, design, applic[...] management, business man[...] his career in Best & Crom[...] Production Engineering an[... in char]ge of production and methods engineering in their pumps division for two years. He then joined Widia India, a German multinational carbide manufacturer where he worked in sales, application engineering, and design of cutting tools for five years. After this stint, he worked at Saint-Gobain Abrasives, where he handled sales, product management, and business management functions for 10 years.

Presently, he is director and CEO at Sabre Learning and Skilling Systems (www.sabre-skilling.com). He is the founder-director of the company, which has trained and skilled over a hundred brands and 65,000 people for 22 years. He has experience in training in India, China, Southeast Asia, the Middle East, and Australia.

He can be contacted at mukund@sabre-skilling.com

Upgrade Your Selling Skills

Don't Sell, Make Them Buy

R. Mukund

Om Books International

Reprinted in 2025

Om Books International

Corporate & Editorial Office
A-12, Sector 64, Noida 201 301
Uttar Pradesh, India
Phone: +91 120 477 4100
Email: editorial@ombooks.com
Website: www.ombooksinternational.com

Sales Office
107, Ansari Road, Darya Ganj,
New Delhi 110 002, India
Phone: +91 11 4000 9000
Email: sales@ombooks.com
Website: www.ombooks.com

Copyright © R. Mukund 2022

ALL RIGHTS RESERVED. The views and opinions expressed in this book are those of the author, and have been verified to the extent possible, and the publishers are in no way liable for the same. No part of this book may be reproduced or transmitted in any form by any means, electronic or mechanical, including photocopying and recording, or by any information storage and retrieval system, except as may be expressly permitted in writing by the publisher.

ISBN: 978-93-92834-71-4

Printed in India

10 9 8

To
Gayathri

Contents

Preface	ix
1. What Is Selling?	1
2. Selling Is a Skill, Not a Process	17
3. Effective Sales Communication	20
4. How To Open And Close a Sale	37
5. How To Connect With Your Customer	49
6. How To Profile the Customer And Build a Rapport	53
7. How To Understand the Needs Of Your Customers	68
8. Value Sell To Customers	85
9. How To Sell To Decision-makers	98
10. How To Handle Customer Concerns	105
11. How To Negotiate With the Customer	121
12. How To Negotiate Successfully	133
13. Make Them Buy	164
Acknowledgements	171

Preface

This book is a tribute to all salespersons who have been relentless in their pursuit of customer acquisition. They frequently face situations with customers where they feel helpless. In addition to their difficulties in selling, they face oversupply of goods, many more competitors, and less spending by customers in the post-Corona era.

Everybody says, "Customers have changed."

Have customers really changed? Many salespeople will tell you that they see umpteen changes in customers' attitudes and behaviour. People essentially remain the same, but what are the major changes that can be seen in customers? They have become increasingly demanding and impatient. They have become very picky about what to buy. They also have a lot of information at their disposal, sometimes more than the person who is selling the product/service to them. The internet and other sources of information as well as the ability to make online purchases has brought about this change in customers. Around 70%–80% of buyers do some amount of research on the internet before buying. They want to buy everything from the comfort of their homes. Another emerging trend in customer behaviour over the last 10–15 years is that quick decisions are being taken by customers. Everything is happening faster now. In order to be effective, salespeople have to pull off in two or three calls what could take 5 to 10 calls earlier. Sales-call-effectiveness measurement is the new measurement index for evaluation of salespeople. It is not about what business you have brought but how fast and in how many calls. The cost of selling has also gone up, and the product lifespan is shorter. So, it is critical for salespeople to skill themselves differently.

This book helps readers to understand human interactions from a salesperson's perspective. It focuses on how to sell and stresses the importance of skill development rather than making sales a step-by-step process. Customers do not like plastic salespersons and interactions that are repetitive and scripted because one approach does not satisfy all customers. Everybody is different and has different and changing needs and the people selling have to understand their customers better and build relationships faster. *Don't Sell, Make Them Buy* focuses on these all-important aspects of selling.

I have spent 22 years in sales and customer service training, and my team has trained over 60,000 salespeople in 3,500 training interventions all over the world, including the USA, Europe, Australia, China, Southeast Asia, the Middle East, and India. In this book, I share the stories and sales situations that my team and I have dealt with. This book offers unique solutions we have developed to sharpen your selling skills. My team and I enjoy meeting customers and we treat each sales call as a challenge to test our skills. The most fascinating thing in sales is that it gives you a chance to meet different types of people, and there is so much to learn from customers in every meeting or call.

Selling is a skill, not a process. Selling skills are constantly changing depending on trends in consumerism. Post-Corona, it is estimated that 95% of sales calls will not be face-to-face, but conference calls. In this digital age where skills for human interaction are dying it is while selling that you are able to develop skills like communication, persuasion, rapport-building, and negotiation.

R. Mukund

1

What Is Selling?

Selling is a process where there is a transaction between two parties—one giving and the other taking. It is often confused with marketing. The 'sales process' is an amazingly simple three-step one. The first step is to understand the needs of the person buying the product. The second is to find the features in your product/service portfolio to satisfy those needs and provide value and benefits. The third, and the most important step, is to build a strong relationship with the person as the first two steps are being executed. Many salespeople think that relationship with the customer is automatically built when their needs are satisfied and they have purchased the product. This is the most dangerous assumption.

Perhaps customers are buying from you as they lack a better choice, or maybe it is convenient for them to buy from you to satisfy a one-time need. Such purchases do not build long-lasting relationships. Hence, in every sales interaction, the salesperson needs to question if they have developed an on-going sustainable relationship with the customer.

How are relationships built? The main ingredient is trust. Similarly, once a customers trusts a salesperson, they blindly buy.

> *Understand the customer's needs. Find features in your product to satisfy those needs. Provide value. Build strong relationships.*

How people buy

People rarely buy products. What does this statement mean? Very often, you notice that customers may have a product in mind but may not be deeply knowledgeable about the specific brand or the features of a product that they want. They often evaluate various brands and compare different available features before they buy. Consumer products, for example, toothpaste or soap, are typical examples where customers get 'locked into' buying. Have these products not changed to meet the changing needs of users? Over the years, you have seen these products undergo a lot of changes regarding their ingredients, shape, variety, benefits, and so on to retain customers.

> *Customers buy a brand for its value to them; trust in it is delivered through the salesperson.*

Customers never stay locked in with one particular brand, like Colgate or Lifebuoy, without a good reason. They are constantly experimenting or stretching their needs. Hence, you can say that they do not buy products any more. They get hooked to a brand instead. "I always buy a Nikon" is a statement a camera enthusiast will often make. Is the customer loyal to the product or the brand? The product here being a camera, and the brand being Nikon. You can see that the brand plays an important role when a customer is buying a product. Nikon has often changed its products to keep its customers satisfied. A leading brand always recognises the changing needs of its customers and builds features to deliver more and more value. The thing to remember is that customers do not buy products. They buy brands.

> *"It used to be that people needed products to survive. Now products need people to survive."*— Nicholas Johnson

What then do customers expect from the salesperson who delivers brand value to them? They expect the salesperson to simplify the benefits of the product and build trust while selling. A salesperson should always keep in mind the fact that customers are buying a brand for its value to them, the capacity of the brand to meet their requirements, and the trust they have in the brand. How do customers evaluate a brand? They evaluate a brand based on their experiences provided by the salespeople, the service people, or e-commerce platforms. This brand image must be reflected in all sales interactions. Salespeople must become the vehicle to deliver the brand image and win the customer's trust.

What is critical to building customer relationship?

All lasting relationships start and end with trust. It is worthwhile to note that when there is ample choice, a buyer will buy happily only if they trust the brand.

Buyers trust the brands they buy, the place at which they are buying, the experience associated with the sales/service interactions, and the touchpoints in the interactions. Touchpoints are what they smell, hear, see, feel, and sense in totality around the buying interactions.

In a sales interaction, the salesperson is constantly being judged by the buyer, and this evaluation is always based on trust. Building trust through sales interactions is the main ingredient of selling.

> *Building trust through sales interactions leads to lasting customer relationships.*

Difference between marketing and selling

While marketing a product or a service, the needs of the target customers are normally understood before making a marketing plan. A marketing person works with the available market research to understand what their target customers want and then decides the product, its price, its positioning, and its placement to deliver value. A salesperson, on the other hand, is given a product, price, and a set of target customers. They must deliver value through relationships. Selling, hence, is often the end point in a marketing activity.

A marketing effort can never be effective till the end point is tied up.

> *Selling is the end point of a marketing activity to deliver value and maintain relationships with buyers. Marketing can never win till the end point is tied up.*

Servicing vs selling

Service is a sales support activity. It is, however, different from selling. In selling, the needs of the customer are not clear, and they either need to be understood or created whereas in servicing, the needs are relatively clear.

Let us take a look at an example of sales and see how it is different from service.

When you walk into an electronics store to buy a new mobile phone, you have many thoughts crowding your mind because of your experiences with your previous mobile phone: *I wish my new mobile has better battery backup. I hope it is not as bulky as my old one. Peter has an iPhone he swears by. I hope such phones are more affordable now. Well, my old phone was not too bad. It has never let me down. At least it was cheap enough. Maybe that is why nobody stole it!*

Will the salesperson ever be able to understand and crystallise all these thoughts and convert them into needs? They can only hope that customers can do it themselves.

The salesperson starts by asking a general question, "What kind of phone would you like, Sir?"

Quite typically, the reaction would be, "I don't know, but what is the current price of an iPhone?"

An effective salesperson is someone who patiently tries to understand what the customer is thinking, clears all their confusion, and converts them into needs. A good salesperson is someone who understands or creates needs in a potential customer and finds ways to satisfy them and build value of the product that they are selling.

> *Selling is about understanding or creating needs in potential customers, satisfying them with benefits, and building lasting relationships with them.*

Now, let us consider an example of servicing.

At an air ticket booking agent's office, a customer walks up to the counter or calls to buy or modify or enquire about a booking. The needs are quite clear. Here, the service person must understand the expectations of the customer. The expectations around a ticketing need may vary from customer to customer. Some are unclear about the ticket they want; some may have an emergency booking. Others may have arrived in a relaxed state, some may walk in agitated. The service person must first understand the expectations of the customer, satisfy these expectations, and then try and exceed them. First, meet the basic expectation and then try to wow the customer.

What if a customer in the office is greeted with, "Good morning, Sir, how are you doing today? Welcome to Air XYZ, this is our welcome drink."

This customer who urgently wants a ticket changed and is likely to miss a flight may be perturbed. The frills are an annoyance at this point.

In both sales and service, interactions with customers are critical to building trust in relationships. Customers are precious especially these days and you always want to do the best you can to make and keep them happy. However, by putting in extra effort to please customers without understanding their expectations or needs, you may end up annoying them and creating an undesirable impact.

What kind of service makes a customer happy? Take a minute to ponder the definition of what qualifies as good service. It is important to note that 'servicing' is different from 'selling'. While selling, you focus on the needs of a customer and try to offer a value to meet their needs. While servicing, needs are normally a given. For example, when someone calls you for a ticketing change, they have already bought a ticket. When you welcome passengers aboard a flight, they have already paid for the flight. When you are waiting to take an order in a restaurant, the customers have already decided to eat there. While cashiering in a retail store, you know that the shoppers have already made up their minds about the things they have picked up from the store.

So, the first step in servicing is to understand the needs, the expectations, and the emotional state of the customer. This is done not just by carefully listening to them. You have to successfully gauge their emotional state of mind. Is the customer looking for an urgent solution or just a clarification? Isn't empathy important when you sense somebody is impatient?

Let me share a deeply personal experience.

A while ago, I received a call from home that my dad had to be urgently admitted in a hospital for respiratory problems. My mother tried her best to manage the situation. And some people rallied around to help. I was stuck in another city and was upset as I knew my mother needed me badly. Though I suspected she needed my help more with managing the crowd that had gathered around to help her.

I headed for the airport at once, desperate to fly to Delhi. I approached a popular airline that I usually fly. I am its platinum club member and have flown 1,50,000 miles with them. As I walked up to the ticket counter, I saw a customer relationship person who looked rather tired.

I was worried, helpless, and angry. "I need a ticket badly... earliest flight out of here."

The airline employee did not look up from the two screens he was working on. "I'm sorry Sir, we are running full on all flights today," he said. "I can get you on a flight tomorrow, the first one out at 5 a.m."

"Hey, please understand my situation. My father was hospitalised today. His condition is serious and he needs me there right now. I fly your airline all the time and I am a platinum card member. Don't I deserve one of those seats you reserve for emergency fliers?"

"Sorry, Sir. We are running full, and we don't expect anybody to drop out as this is the weekend."

I backed off, frustrated beyond words. I went to the next counter where I spotted a staff member who was smiling. Seeing my agitated state, her expression changed from a smile to one of empathy.

"Do you have a flight to Delhi tonight?" I asked.

"I'm so sorry, Sir, we are a small airline and we fly only thrice every day. However, please wait..." She checked her computer and made a call.

"I am really sorry you can't fly with us," she informed me. "But I checked and got to know that you can fly with that airline", pointing three counters away. "They have a few seats on the flight departing in an hour. Hope it will suit you."

She could clearly sense what my expectations were and knew that I was very distressed. I was immensely grateful.

I rushed to the counter and bought my tickets. As I waited for my flight, I wondered whether I will ever fly with my old airline again. Will it ever be my first choice?

Good service is about understanding expectations of the customer and putting in your best efforts to meet them. You can exceed expectations of the customer only after you meet their basic expectations.

Service is a skill, and it needs to be embellished with the correct attitude.

> *Servicing is about understanding customer's expectations around needs, meeting these expectations, and then trying to exceed them to make the customer happy.*

What is consumerism?

Consumerism is a social and economic order that encourages the buying of goods and services in ever-increasing amounts. It is triggered by people buying the things they want. When, how, and why do consumers buy products? This question has plagued marketing and salespeople for centuries because brands are always trying to acquire loyal customers. Consumers buy when they need, want or desire products or services. What is the difference between need, want, and desire?

A need is generated in a customer when they cannot do without something. When it is an element of their lifestyle that they cannot do without.

A want is generated when a customer does not need something, but still goes ahead and buys it. Their buying may be triggered by the need to flaunt a new product. Or a style factor a customer feels that they must indulge in.

A desire is generated around a customer's aspirations and these are constantly growing. A luxury brand spurs people's desires.

> *Consumerism is normally triggered by addressing the needs, wants, and desires of consumers.*

Philip Kotler, widely known as the father of modern marketing, has remarkably interesting points to make on the post-Corona era of consumerism. He has interesting observations to share about the new attitudes and behavioural changes in consumers. In the pre-Corona era, he says, "Consuming became a lifestyle", whereas in the post-Corona era, there will evolve a new consumer trait that is bound to influence spending. He says this new spending will be triggered by "life simplifiers".

Before Corona, shoppers were willing to indulge themselves and buy freely. They wanted to spend on things they did not need. Spurred by a reason to flaunt and show off a lifestyle.

People and businesses are threatened more than ever now. The sources of wealth creation are not the same as before. At such a time, people tend to hold back their spending. Wants and desires will relegate to needs, and people will buy what they absolutely need. Over the last few years, people have already become careful spenders and stopped buying merely products. They bought brands they trusted. Today, they may not even buy the brands they trusted before. They will look for something else—something that is deeply linked with trust. They will start buying a brand culture. Before buying, they will raise questions about a brand along the following lines—What does it stand for? What is the purpose of the brand? How do people associated with it reflect those brand values?

Brands must redefine their value propositions, or a promise by a company to a customer. Brands need to be IMPACTFUL to attract and retain customers.

Brands need to redefine what they stand for. When presenting their products and the brands, they need to ensure that they are 'culture embedded'. This means when a customer is buying a brand, they would be eager to know what values it reflects and how it is contributing to society.

What is customer acquisition?

When can you say that you have acquired a customer?

Most salespeople will say that they have acquired a customer when they have sold something to them. Yes, there has been a commercial transaction, and the customer has paid for the product and bought it. Does that mean that the sale is over?

In the case of some products, some after-sales service will be needed. This could be installation or maintenance and support. For some products such as food and home consumables, the customer may need to make a repeat buy. You also need to keep in mind customer advocacy, which involves the customer advocating that the product be bought by others, hence, drawing in more customers.

So, a customer is not acquired when a sale is made. In fact, the sale has just started at this point. The first sale is sometimes called a trial order. The customer is experimenting with what they have bought. This is when the salesperson must be careful and start building value. Building value merely means that customers are satisfied, and convinced that there is value for the money they spent. They are happy they bought something worthwhile. It is very important to ensure that the customer does not feel cheated or does not feel like returning or badmouthing the product. The avenues for expressing such grievances are many these days. In fact, it can be done at the flick of a button on social media sites, blogs, and chat boxes.

Hence, the salespeople of today must start feeling more and more concerned after the first sale. Over time, they must make sure the customer relationship is strengthened, and they must work hard to be a nodal reference point in their community and field of influence. The customer's testimony is more important than the purchase order today.

This is a tall order! In fact, it is exceedingly difficult to meet expectations, let alone exceed them, while acquiring customers.

> *You can never say that you have acquired a customer just by making a sale. The customer's testimony is more important than the purchase order.*

We are all aware of the sales motto that the customer is always right. Let me quote a relevant story that I read on a news portal:

A lady owned a sandwich shop in a small town. A customer once complained that her soup was too hot. The lady apologised immediately and explained that they had to keep it hot according to the health codes. "Well," said the customer. "I've been coming here for over a year, and I've never burned my lips on having your soup before, and I have now. Maybe there is something wrong with your equipment."

The owner told her that was impossible, as the warmer was only six months old. "And so is my restaurant," she added.

The customer never came back.

Can you ever say that you have happy customers and that they are fully acquired? If the customer is always right and you are always wrong as a salesperson, can you survive in any business?

Yes and no. It really boils down to the cost of selling and servicing; the cost of adding value in selling. Does the value in the product justify the extra service or selling effort and costs? Can you customise your products to the different needs of the customer? All six billion customers have six billion needs. Then, products would need six billion features.

So, what will make a customer happy in a relationship and when can you feel that the customer has been acquired?

It is perfectly simple, really. Customers' needs and expectations keep changing constantly. Keeping in touch with customers is the first step in keeping them happy, or at least ensuring that they stay in the relationship. It is the small things you need to do in the relationship that matter. There can never be a process or a formula for this because everybody is wired differently and expects differently. It is not just product knowledge or the expertise in what you sell that will help you. There must be the congruence of your mind and heart, and how they mesh.

The following story will help to make my point clearer.

An 89-year-old man was snowed in at his Pennsylvania home during the winter holidays, and his daughter who lived out of town was worried that he was not going to have access to enough food due to the impending storm and the bad weather. After calling multiple stores in a desperate attempt to find someone who would deliver to her father's home, she finally got through to someone at Joe's Diner, who told her that the diner did not accept home deliveries.

However, given the extremely difficult circumstances, the employee told her that they would gladly deliver directly to her father's home, and even suggested additional items that would fit in perfectly with his special low-sodium diet.

After the daughter placed the order, the employee told her that she need not worry about the price as the food would be delivered free of charge. The employee then wished her a Merry Christmas and hung up.

Within half an hour the food was at the man's doorstep—for free!

In refusing to let red tape get in the way of a customer in need, Joe's Diner showed that customer service is not about generating fanfare. It can simply be about doing the right thing.

> *There is no fully satisfied customer. There is only a win–win customer relationship that makes both parties happy.*

Stages of customer acquisition

Building customer relationship and retaining them is an ongoing process. The salespeople of today must pursue customers relentlessly till they are acquired and retained.

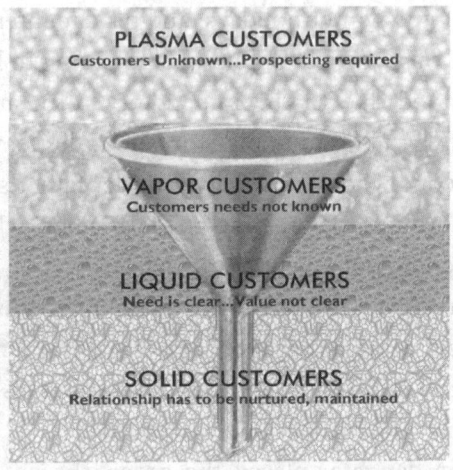

There are four phases of customer developments leading to acquisition and retaining customers.

Some salespeople refer to their customers as 'old customers' and 'new customers'. This is not a good way of categorising them. There may be customers who do not know you, and customers who have just learnt about you, or whom you have just learnt about. These are **plasma customers**. There are customers who have heard about you and your products. You also know they need your products. However, they do not know whether it will benefit them to buy anything from you. These are **vapour customers**. Then, there are customers who have almost decided, but not quite. They are unsure of the value they will get from your products. These customers need to be convinced. These are **liquid customers**. Possibly, they need to sample and test. Finally, there are customers who see value and have been steadily buying. These are **solid customers**. They need to be nourished or else, they will move away. Thus at no stage can you say that a customer is fully acquired.

The concept of tracking which type of customer you are dealing with is called sales funnelling. Often, a good salesperson allocates time for selling to different types of customers. Some pay more attention to plasma customers, and some to solid customers. It depends on the status of the relationship and the time available. That is, salespeople feel that the work done by them to bring customers to this stage is enough for the customers to buy. They do not spend enough time on explaining the value of the product they are selling more effectively. As a rule of thumb, salespeople need to spend 60% of their time with customers who are in the vapour stage and liquid stage and 40% of their time with plasma and solid stage customers.

Are you not selling every day?

You sell every day but many fear selling. It is like a phobia. "I can never be good at it," "Not my cup of tea"—these are some of the remarks you will keep hearing.

People are hesitant to take up a sales job because it is very target-driven and involves handling a complex set of people almost daily to meet your numbers. Customers are becoming more and more demanding these days. And Covid-19 has made it worse and messed up people's minds. "Nobody wants anything these days"—this is another complaint you often hear.

Let us take a step back and contemplate. Are you not selling every day? To your parents, your children, your friends, bosses, and colleagues. You sell an idea, a favour, something you badly want done, etc.

Selling is not that complex. Neither is it a performing art, such as singing or dancing, which requires relentless practice and effort. It is an art, nevertheless. It is the art of winning over people by engaging, persuading, negotiating, and ultimately winning their trust and building relationships.

Says Chad T. Dyar, author of *How to Talk to Humans*, "These days, everyone, in every line of work, must sell at some point. Job candidates need to 'sell' themselves to be hired. Managers need to sell ideas to higher-ups. CEOs need to sell initiatives such as strategic plans to their boards."

You need to be good at selling to win in life.

Nowadays, social media is where perceptions are formed and opinions are firmed up. Hence, every single person in an organisation needs to sell today. Earlier, it was the restricted domain of the sales team. When a product is launched and marketing plans are put in place, salespeople should not be the only ones who need to gear up for selling. All employees of the organisation have to have a deep understanding of sales and marketing to start powering the product in their own spheres of influence.

The fault in the thinking of people in many organisations is that revenues are driven by the sales team and the sales team alone. Organisations put in a lot of energy into hiring the best salespeople they can afford, training them on their product or service, and then letting them loose and hoping for the best. The problem with this thinking is that salespeople are only one part of the equation. Everybody's efforts go into making a product, so shouldn't everybody be engaged in selling?

2

SELLING IS A SKILL, NOT A PROCESS

The sales toolbox is a set of steps using the following techniques:
1. Opening
2. Probing
3. Supporting/Presenting
4. Handling objections
5. Closing

It is often thought that a good salesperson should open the sale, probe to understand the customer's needs, support the needs with product features-advantages-benefits, handle the customer's questions, and close the sale. This process is time-tested and works well. So, a person who follows these steps should be able to sell very well, right?

Well, it was possible and remarkably effective when customers lacked knowledge about the various options available to them in the market, did not clearly know what their needs were, and preferred to stay loyal to a limited number of brands and products. But the internet provides a host of information to customers about what is available and how they could upgrade the products that they are currently using. However, too much of information has rendered customers confused. With too much choice they are not able to decide what is best suited for them. They are not open to discussing their problems with salespersons.

Customers are also reluctant to spare enough time for salespeople to understand their needs and meet their requirements. They do not encourage the free flow of information, are overly cautious about product changes, and evaluate the price of products critically. Who is not driven towards cost reduction? Product lifecycles are also becoming shorter, and there is a need to be flexible, fast, and constantly open to changes in sales approaches to succeed in selling.

This changing scenario has put demands on salespeople for newer skills. While the reliable and time-tested sales toolbox works, salespeople should constantly evolve to enhance their skills and selling tactics to keep winning in sales. At this point, I am reminded of a resourceful salesman:

I went to a Volkswagen showroom and a VW Polo caught my eye. It was the cheapest car in the forecourt.

The salesman said, "Get in here and start her up."

Well, I got in and put my foot down and crashed straight into a luxury car. I just did not realise the cars were left in gear. I put my head in my hands, and there was a stunned silence.

The salesman tapped me on the shoulder and said, "Are you all right, mate? To be fair, accidents happen, and to be fair, the Polo hasn't come out of this too badly."

I noticed he was limping as he asked, "Shall I get the logbook to book the order?"

I asked, "Have I just run over your foot?"

He whimpered, "Yeah, you did, and it is throbbing a bit, but to be fair, I have had worse injuries playing football."

It was not until I got home that the humour of the incident hit me. Some always look on the bright side of life. This salesman was definitely one of them. He sold a car on the basis of a sad story, generated sympathy, and must have told the same story and showed his bruised leg to 10 other customers, and managed to sell five more cars.

3

Effective Sales Communication

In the first chapter, you understood the importance of sales interactions which first builds trust and then relationships. Sales communication techniques are important to enhance the quality of interactions between the buyer and the seller, and thus build rapport. Only by building rapport will you gain trust of the buyer. In this chapter, you will learn more about the various kinds of sales communication.

These are:
- Face-to-face interactions
- Telephone calls
- Videoconferencing
- Emails, letters, proposals, quotations, texting, voice mails

In all sales communication, you must keep in mind the person with whom you are communicating. The sender may be the same, however, the receiver keeps changing. All people are not the same when it comes to processing communications. A standard way of communicating with all customers is also not desirable when you want to build trust and relationships with them. So, what is the best way of communicating in sales situations? And what are the basic elements of communication?

Why is rapport an all-important factor?

You need to build rapport to make a good first impression. You must make an impression so that:

- You catch people's attention.
- You get them interested in what you are saying.
- You make them trust what you say.
- You make them bond with you so that they can divulge more information about themselves.

Thus, generating rapport is the starting point of any relationship especially between sellers and buyers. It is easy to generate rapport with people we like because our elements for communicating are already tuned. Birds of a feather flock together. A rapport is easily created between people who share common interests. The difficulty is in generating rapport with unknown people or with those who you do not like. When two people meet each other for the first time, rapport is not immediately built because they are sensing and feeling each other's space and auras. Only when they are comfortable with each other will rapport be generated.

You need to be conscious about how you are generating rapport, as you cannot sell without building a rapport with the customer. You will learn a lot about how to create rapport with different people and their specific personalities in later chapters.

> *Rapport leads to trust. Trust leads to relationships.*

First impressions

You often hear the phrase, "the first impression is the last impression", which means that the first impression you make

> *A standard way of communicating with all customers is not desirable for building rapport, trust, and relationships.*

Elements of communication

There are primarily three mediums through which you communicate:
- Your body language
- Your voice
- The words you use

Let us first see why all three are important. You communicate primarily to build rapport and then trust. What is rapport? It is a kind of frequency match between two people, which then goes on to build trust. How to build a rapport?

Simply put, you must change your behaviour by controlling your body language, voice, and words to suit the the person you are interacting with. Sometimes, all this is done involuntarily or from practice.

> *The three elements through which rapport is built are body language, voice, and words.*

From the time you were born, you have been communicating, sometimes correctly, sometimes not-so-correctly. Communicating comes naturally to us. At least, that is what we tend to believe.

But my personal take is that animals communicate better than human beings. Watch some well-made wildlife shows on TV and you will agree with me on this count.

on people is often what they carry back with them. Some would say, "The first impression is the lasting impression." You do get chances later on to change the impression people have about you, but they will certainly carry a bit of the first impression in their minds for good.

When first-time salespeople meet prospective customers, they must ask themselves, "How do I make the first impression count?"

The other thing that most people worry about is how to make a good first impression when they do not know the person they are meeting. The worry around building a rapport with a stranger is mostly due to fear and lack of preparation. One good way to get rid of your fear is to do some background research on the prospective customer you are trying to impress. You can do this by checking their online profiles. It is very common to do so these days. But be careful; never assume anything about a person.

> *The first impression is the lasting impression. Make it count.*

How do you build a rapport?

You can generate rapport by applying your sensory abilities first to observe the way people are behaving and then changing your sensory behaviours to suit them. We are programmed over years to develop a sensory ability to observe certain behaviours in people and we change ourselves to respond and match them. For example, if you see somebody smiling at you, you may interpret that as a friendly behaviour. While others would sense this as the other person wanting something from them and hence is trying to be friendly. You can generate rapport by first observing the way people are behaving and then changing your behaviour to suit them.

Observe the customer's body language, voice, and words, and try to match them. So, how do you match in each of these? If the customer has an expressive face and you have a deadpan one, you will not create rapport. So, start displaying some expressions to show that you want to be like the customer in this aspect. If the customer's voice is high-pitched and their way of speaking is fast, and you have a soft-pitched voice and a slower pace of speech, try and raise your pitch and speed to say, "I want to be like you." If the customer uses formal language, you try and include such kinds of words in your dialogue with them.

What you are trying to do here is 'match' or say, "I want to be like you." You will start creating a rapport then.

> *Change your behaviour to suit the person you are building a rapport with; match the body language, voice, and word cues that you are receiving.*

A few examples of how to match and create rapport are given below. It is, however, important to note that while matching to create rapport, you are not mirroring. The person with whom you are trying to build a rapport should not feel that you are imitating them. It should be done subtly.

Effective Sales Communication

Body language	
Customer makes strong eye contact.	Make more eye contact than you usually do.
Customer has an expressive face and expresses emotions felt clearly.	Add more gestures such as nodding, smiling, softening your gaze.
Customer uses many hand gestures.	Start using your hands to communicate but make sure the gestures are respectful.
Customer's posture is correct and proper.	Adopt a proper posture and display enthusiasm.
Voice	
Customer has a fast rate of speech.	Increase your rate of speech with short sentences and lesser pauses between sentences and key words.
Customer has a slow rate of speech.	Slow down and increase pauses between sentences and key words.
Customer has a high pitch in voice.	Raise your pitch from your normal one—add more volume to your voice.
Words	
Customer uses technical words.	Try and use technical words.
Customer uses respectful phrases.	Use only formal, respectful phrases.
Customer uses slang expressions.	Use respectful and friendly words, avoid slang.

Importance of listening while selling

Listening is the most important skill needed in sales. As Stephen E. Heiman says in his book, *New Conceptual Selling*, selling is 80% listening and 20% talking. If you have listened well to your customer, most tasks will be easy in sales, including generating rapport with them. However, listening is not easy, and it is a cultivated skill. Around two million bits/seconds worth of information bombard our five senses—sight, hearing, taste, touch, and smell, and we receive a total of 134 bits of it. Only 0.01% of what we are capable of receiving is actually received and processed.

It is interesting to note how the word 'listening' is depicted in Mandarin. In Chinese, a combination of letters or words makes up individual words. The word 'listening' is made up of four words—ears, eyes, heart, and mind (undivided attention).

Normally, we start our analysis as we are listening. This is where most listening mistakes begin. As we are listening and analysing, our ability to listen decreases since the mind is occupied in processing what we are listening.

The human mind can be compared to the random-access memory (RAM) in a computer's central processing unit (CPU). If the RAM is busy processing tasks, it cannot store information to analyse or process more tasks. Listening requires mental space and undivided attention. What this really means for a salesperson is—do not be distracted when the customer is speaking to you. Just listen with undivided attention.

> **Listen with your ears, eyes, mind (undivided attention), and heart.**

Listening with your heart simply means that you are in the customer's emotional space as you are listening. If the customer is explaining a happy situation, you need to feel and reflect the pleasant emotion using a smile. If the customer is relating a sad situation, you need to feel and show genuine empathy. If the customer is seriously explaining something important, you need to have an intense listening expression such as open eyes and frequent nodding to encourage them. This is what it means to listen with your heart.

An easy way of listening better while selling is to have a clean sheet of paper in front of you as you are listening and noting down the keywords. Underline the words about which you need more clarity so that questions can be asked later. Do not spend time pondering what has been said. Do not interrupt a customer while they are speaking. It is advisable to give a two-second gap before you respond to a customer. This is to ensure that the customer has completed what they were saying.

Pioneering neuroscientist Stephen Heinemann calls this gap a "golden silence".

> *Do not just listen to the customer's words. Listen to their emotions as well.*

How to use the elements of communication

You know that the three elements in sales communication are body language, voice, and words. While communicating with a customer, at least during the first minute or so, body language is what they notice the most (making 58% impact), followed by voice (making 32% impact), and then words (making 10% impact). This shows that the customer is more swayed by body language and voice than words.

Let us see how you can control these three elements consciously and use them effectively while communicating.

Body language elements	What to control
Your smile	Full smile for greeting or acknowledging a happy situation.
	Half smile to indicate politeness and to mean 'I have nothing to add'.

Your eyes	Make your eyes wide when listening to something important.
	Narrow your eyes when you are smiling.
	Soften your gaze when you are greeting or acknowledging the customer.
	Make soft eye contact. Do not stare into the customer's eyes. Look at the eye zone softly.
Your face	Master the right facial expressions for pleasantly wishing the customer, showing empathy, being assertive, and listening—and use them appropriately.
Your posture while standing	Stand erect while greeting, and bend forward while listening.
Your hands	Keep your hands in front of your body, when greeting or listening to the customer face to face.
	Never point with your index finger or keep your thumbs pointing outwards while gesturing.
	Avoid raising your hands above your chest while gesturing.

Your feet	Your feet should never be apart and should be always as close to each other as possible.
Your posture while sitting	Always sit with your knees together.
	Keep your feet below your knees to maintain an erect posture while listening.
	Place your hands in front, on the table, visible to customers.
	Keep your elbows off the table.

Body language: what to control

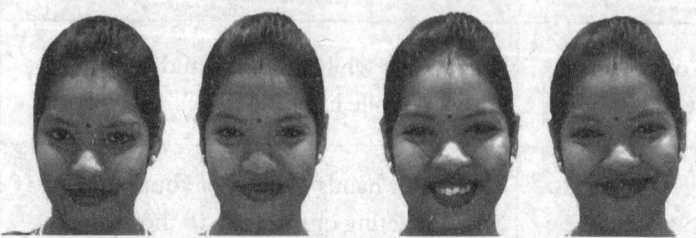

A full smile indicates willingness to genuinely care about building a relationship. It also indicates keenness to share. Whatever mood you may be in, a smile should be the starting point when you meet a person. It is advisable to practice this till you get it right.

The half-smile indicates that you are not really concerned with what you feel or say. It shows less openness to share. It is also the expression you use when you want to discourage the other person if something rude or unpleasant is being said.

The 'no' smile indicates that you are not really interested in building a relationship.

It shows the salesperson's unwillingness to share information. It should be avoided in all sales interactions.

Sitting with your hands folded while listening to a customer can indicate that you are the boss, and that you do not want to get closer in the relationship. Sitting back in your chair with your legs spread out indicates a casual approach. Putting your elbows on the table sends a signal that you are controlling, or trying to control the situation.

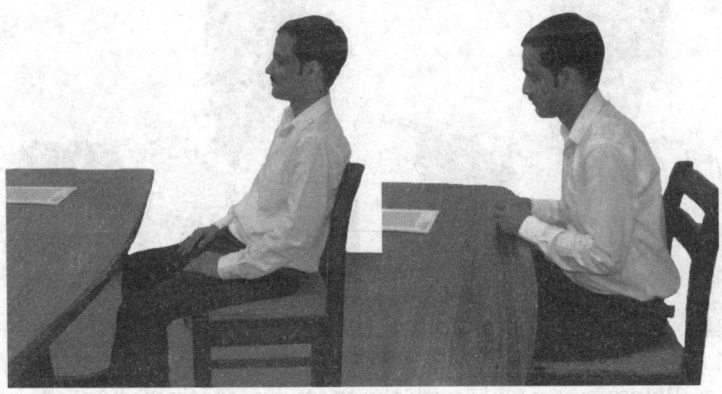

Sitting with only your hands visible (elbows off the table) on the table indicates your seriousness in building the relationship. It also shows that you have a positive outlook about the discussion.

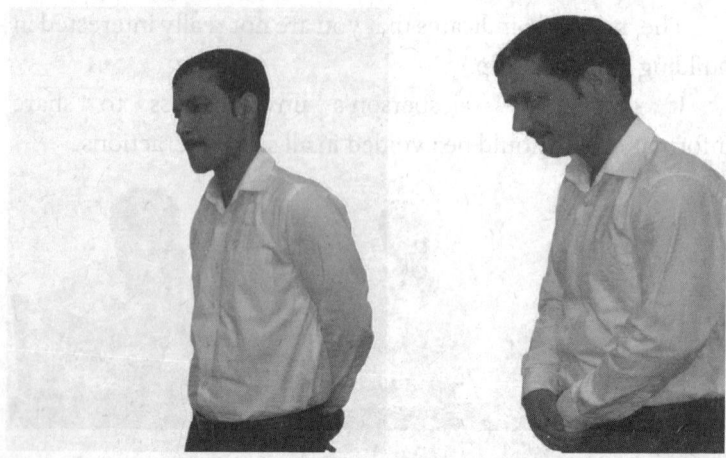

While reposing or waiting (the customer may be busy speaking to someone else), it is better to wait attentively, keeping your hands in front of you. Hands at the back posture while waiting signals disinterest, which can be picked up by the customer.

Pointing at people with the index finger is rude and often read as insolent behaviour.

Pointing while using an open-hand gesture is considered respectful.

Pointing at objects with the index finger is also considered rude. It is advisable to use an open-hand, two-finger pointing gesture.

Some of the communication aspects given so far are not easy to master, especially in a subconscious way. It requires a lot of practice and repeated attempts to get them right. One way to start mastering them is to stand before a mirror, and work on your facial expressions, smile, and postures. Keep tweaking your expressions till you are satisfied and then start using them. Remember, it takes 200 hours of conscious practice to form a habit. Being conscious of your body language is, however, the first step towards mastering your body language.

> *Check your expressions in a mirror and keep improving them till you are satisfied. It takes 200 times of conscious practice to form a habit.*

Voice: what to control

If the body language is difficult to control, voice is an even more difficult thing to master. You must make serious efforts to use the correct voice for the correct situation. Voice control is becoming increasingly important in sales situations nowadays because you are not meeting customers face-to-face that frequently but calling them on the phone or videoconferencing with them. In such situations, your voice plays a particularly important role, and becomes a substitute for your body language.

Do we have different voices? Do we really need to use a particular voice for face-to-face interactions and another for phone calls? These are some of the questions that may come to mind as you try and understand your communication needs.

Let us try to understand what these different voices are and when you tend to use them.

There are primarily four types of voices that you use.

The **soft voice** is a voice where the words are formed in your mouth, and you do not throw your voice. That means not much air is thrown with the voice. The soft voice is used for communication when you need to be soft and respectful, and you are in close proximity to the customer. It can also be used while making a telephone call.

The **full voice** is a voice in which words are mixed with a lot of air, while the speaker exhales from the chest. The speaker breathes sufficiently well through the nose and exhales with the voice. Yoga teaches pranayama, a breathing exercise that enriches the voice. It can be practised by chanting, 'Om', which was traditionally used in *gurukuls* (ancient Indian residential schooling system). This voice is richer, has a lot of throw, and is normally used when the telephone line is noisy or when speaking to a larger audience seated in a huge space or room. This voice is also used when you are speaking about your products in detail and trying to demonstrate your confidence in being of service to the customer. This voice can be cultivated by a set of breathing exercises. Public speakers and people who use their voices a lot like professional singers should use their full voice.

The **shriek voice** has a high pitch and frequency. You tend to use it if you are in the habit of speaking fast. This voice should certainly be avoided in phone calls since it will make you sound as if you are upset. When this voice is used for a long time, it causes coughing sensations and throat-clearing sounds. Try and avoid using this voice as far as possible. If you cannot avoid it, try to make shorter sentences and breathe frequently when you pause. This will ensure that your voice sounds richer than it is.

The **base voice** is the one that is generated from the belly. This voice is used when you have to assert yourself, especially when you have to say no.

Given below is a list that specifies when to use the four types of voices.

Soft voice	When you stand close to the customer.
	When telephone lines are clear.
	When you empathise.
	When you must share a not-so happy news.
Full voice—air-filled voice	When you make a group presentation.
	When you must show confidence.
	When you talk about your products and service capabilities.
	When there is ambient noise in a room or on a call.
Shriek voice—shrill voice	Avoid as much as possible.
Base voice	When you must assert yourself.
	When you have to say no to customers.

Words: what to control

While selling, you should always give a lot of thought to and emphasis on the words you use. Try and observe the words used by the customer and make an effort to use similar words. Always behave and speak professionally when you do not know the customer well and you have to start a conversation. Make sure the words being used are always respectful. Remember, during selling, you are always trying to build a professional relationship. I am not a great fan of using standard phrases like "Good Morning" "I understand" "Sorry to keep you waiting", as they tend to sound very impersonal and cold. Still, you must ensure that the words you use are not crude, personal, arrogant, or overfriendly as they may not reflect the brands that you are selling.

One way to ensure that the right words are used is to note down keywords used by the customer when you are listening and include them in your conversation. It also helps if you keep a checklist of respectful words that can be used in the various languages you employ while selling.

> *Body language makes the most impact, followed by voice, and then words for creating first impressions. It is not what you do or say, but how you do or say them that counts.*

4

How To Open and Close a Sale

What is 'opening' in a sale? Opening refers to the first conversation you have with a customer whether it's face-to-face or on a call. The first few sentences are extremely critical. We have already discussed that the first impression is the lasting impression. Personally, whenever I am planning to make a sales call, I always take pains to plan the call and write down the keywords for the first few sentences. Normally salespeople start to converse without a plan, and then they get stuck. Just as opening a call is important, planning how to open the call is crucial too. What you must plan depends on the call, whether it is the first time you are calling (or meeting) the customer, and the context of the call. It is always essential to plan in advance. A good opening is possible only when you are prepared.

Pre-opening—greetings and introductions

Pre-opening refers to what you must do before making a sales pitch. Before you open in sales, greet the customer.

How greetings are exchanged differs from country to country and place to place. However, what is said while greeting is not so important as how it is said. Greeting is 100% body language and tone of the voice. I have heard many body language experts stress on the fact that for the first 15 seconds, a customer does not hear you as they are busy sensing and feeling you. So, body language and voice control are critical. What specific aspects of body language are important when you greet a person? Normally, a customer notices your facial expressions, your posture, and the tone of your voice. Let us analyse how the above aspects are important during greeting.

Four most important aspects in a greeting:

- Eye contact
- The smile
- The nod
- The handshake

Eye contact

The eyes reflect emotion and thus play a very important part in communication. When you make eye contact with your customer, the gaze needs to be soft, showing no aggression. How do you make your gaze soft? By making sure that you smile. Making eyeball-to-eyeball contact can make a customer feel that there is aggression in your greeting.

I am reminded of a salesperson in a luggage store who once told me, "Sir, yesterday I practised the skill of making eye contact while greeting my customers. One of the customers, a girl, slapped me. She accused me of staring at her."

It is extremely important to make your gaze soft while greeting a customer and not make eyeball-to-eyeball contact. Look around the customer's eye zone and softly into their eyes.

One way is to narrow your eyes and look between the customer's eyes. The best way to practise eye contact in greeting is to look at yourself in the mirror and greet yourself with a softened gaze at least 10 times every day for a month. You will find your best eye contact and the smile that goes well with greetings. Like I always say, it takes 200 times of practice to make a habit.

> *Practise eye contact, your smile, and your nod at least 200 times to make them perfect.*

The smile

The next step in a greeting is your smile. Your smile must be full and genuine while greeting a potential customer. A half-smile is a passive one that tells the customer, "I am just doing my job and I have no intention of building a relationship with you."

The nod

The third step in a greeting is the nod. Nodding signifies that you respect the other person. This is done extremely well in the East, specially China, Japan, and Southeast Asia. Nodding after smiling (just a small nod will do), adds respect to the greeting.

So, to sum up, a greeting has three components for you to master:
Step 1 Soft eye contact
Step 2 A full smile, which is genuine not plastic
Step 3 A gentle nod to say I respect you

The handshake

Internationally, the handshake has been the most preferred form of greeting, at least for official meetings. People have different styles of shaking hands. Each type of handshake communicates something different to the customer. The namaste with a nod is used in many parts of Asia. Without the nod, namaste is imperfect.

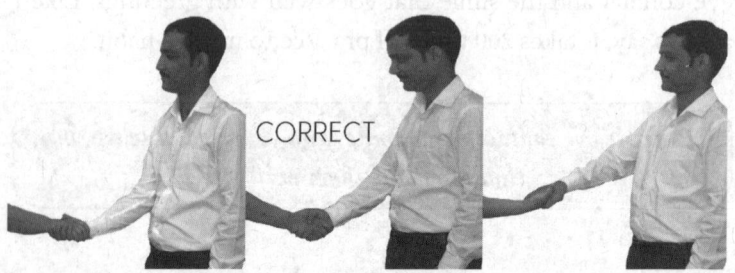

CORRECT

Some handshakes and what they can communicate are given below:

Type of handshake	What they communicate
Above the chest handshake	I want to dominate you.
Faraway handshake	I do not want to build a relationship with you.
Too close a handshake	I want to get close to you—personally.
Open palm handshake	I would like you to accept what I am giving or saying.
Closed palm handshake	I am forcing you to take what I am giving or suggesting.
Gripping handshake	I'm always controlling.
Loose handshake	I'm not confident.

The best handshake or the safest way to shake hands without incurring the risk of the customer forming a wrong opinion about you is to shake hands straight, closer to the belly, at just the right distance, move forward if required, slide your hands to make web-to-web contact (the 'web' is the curved expanse of space from the top of your thumb to the tip of your index finger), wait for the customer to shake your hand and judge if the handshake is strong or weak. Matching the pressure of the customer's palm signifies that you want a partnership in the relationship.

To sum up:

Judge the distance to shake hands when moving forward—make the effort to get around the conference table if the table is big.

Maintain eye contact and smile to show confidence.

Ensure your handshake is below the chest, and move your upper torso forward a little if required.

Slide in your hands to make web-to-web contact and judge the pressure.

Match the pressure and release after one or two shakes.

Keep practising your handshake to perfect it.

The positive handshake is straight with bent elbows, and shaken below the waist area. You need to bend or move forward to perfect your handshake.

The closed-palm handshake is palm down and indicates that you are in control.

The open-palm handshake is palm up and indicates that you are giving away your control.

The faraway handshake with the straight elbow indicates that you are not too interested in building a relationship.

Introductions on a call

When meeting new people, you greet them first and then introduce yourself. The important aspects to consider in an introduction are who are you, what is the brand you represent, and how it will benefit the person you are meeting. I have found that many salespersons introduce themselves as representing a company or a distributor. As far as the customer is concerned, they buy brands and benefits in products. They are not so concerned about who is bringing the brand to them. Let us consider a situation where a salesman who is working for Evershine, a distributor of Samsonite products and how he introduces himself to a customer. If he says "I am Thomas, I am from Samsonite," it makes more sense to the customer than if he says "I am Thomas from Evershine Distributors." In the first case, he is introducing the brand rather than the distributor he represents. This will gain him more respect from the customer. Even if the salesman is working for the distributor of Samsonite, he should introduce the brand (Samsonite) that he represents first.

While introducing yourself, you could hand out your visiting card to the customer. This can be done before or after the introduction. Never introduce yourself while the customer is reading the card, as they may not be listening well enough to remember your name or the brand you represent. While introducing yourself, use a name that is easy for the customer to remember. This is important when you have a long or complicated name.

After you have introduced yourself tell the customer about the benefits of the brand, or what you can offer to the customer which is beneficial. "I'm Phillip from Castrol, and our division offers a wide range of industrial lubricants for machine tools," is better than saying, "I'm Phillip from GG lubricants. We deal in Castrol."

To sum up introductions:
1. **Who are you**—Your name, which is easy for customers to remember.
2. **The brand** you represent.
3. **The benefit** or what you are offering which may be of interest to the customer.

It is particularly important to remember that while greetings and introductions are being done, you need to maintain eye contact with the customer. You should also use a strong full voice, and keywords such as name and brand name should be stressed and modulated. Remember, this is the phase when the customer is judging you and deciding whether to give you a full hearing or not.

Opening the sale

Once the pre-opening is done, it is time to open the sale. While opening, tell the customer the purpose of your call and the agenda. All calls, whether telephonic or face-to-face, need a call objective. What is a call objective and what is the difference between 'objectives' and 'actions'?

A call objective is the outcome you are expecting from the call. An action is a list of things you need to do in the call to meet your call objective. The list of things to do should be planned keeping the call objective in mind. Sometimes, calls could have more than one objective.

After the objective and actions are finalised, it is important to pick the keywords you are going to use in the call. This will increase your confidence while opening correctly. Remember, opening lines must be crisp—less than 15 words in total. It is better if you write down your opening lines for first calls/meetings and rehearse them to get the opening right, so that you are able to project a lot of confidence. If you fumble for words as you are making the opening, you will lose confidence as you go on.

> *All calls, whether they are telephonic or face-to-face, must have a call objective.*

Let us look at a simple call plan and the opening line for a housing project.

Objective or Agenda	Actions	Keywords
Understand the customer's home requirements.	Find out how many family members are there. Carry the popular house plans you have designed.	Come to meet. To **present** our **house plans.**
	Carry a portfolio of photos of houses you have made. Find out their budget without asking directly. Ask about their location preferences.	We have a **wide range** from $25,000 to $550,000. Flexible options.

A simple way of opening in a face-to-face meeting after pre-opening and introductions would be: "I have come to understand your home requirements and present our wide range of house plans with flexible options."

You can see that the opening has 15 words, which were written down from the call planner. With this kind of opening, the customer will become mentally ready to answer the questions you come up with during the rest of the interaction. The customer is also clear regarding the purpose of your visit. When you are confident about which words to use, you will also sound confident in your opening line.

After opening, you normally request either the customer's time, or, if the customer has already given you time, thank them for it.

So, a proper opening could be worded as, "I have come to understand your home requirements and present our wide range of house plans with flexible options. I hope you could spare 10 minutes for me, please."

This will tell the customer precisely what you need from them. If the customer is busy, the time could be rescheduled.

If the meeting has already been fixed through a call, then the lines could be: "Thank you for giving me the time to meet you. I have come to meet you to understand your home requirements and present our wide range of house plans and flexible options."

Time is the most precious commodity today, and by respecting your customer's time, you are giving the person a signal that you value their time. Depending on the time given by the customer, the agendas you have planned can be prioritised.

> *Time is the most precious commodity today, and by respecting your customer's time, you are giving the person a signal that you value them.*

Pre-opening and opening in telephonic calls

This is similar to what we have discussed for face-to-face calls. The only difference is that you must concentrate not on body language but on your voice modulation to make an impact. There are minor differences in the way a phone call needs to be scripted. Let us take the example of a call to a prospective customer called Mr Thomas who is looking to buy a new home.

Introductory wish	Good morning!
Identifying the person	Am I speaking to Mr Thomas, please?
Response	Yes.
Greet the person	Good morning, Mr Thomas!
Introduction	My name is Peter; I am calling from Lakeside Homes.
Opening	I am calling to fix a meeting to understand your home requirements and show you our plans.
Requesting time	Is this a good time to speak?

What would happen if you say, "I am Sharon calling from X Bank. Is this a good time to speak?" The response would normally be to retreat and say no because the customer will think you are trying to sell them something they do not need and get a feeling that you may be pushy when you say more.

So, the ideal way of opening would be to include the agenda in the opening and then going on to request time. For instance, "Good morning, Sir! I'm Sharon calling from X Bank. This is regarding a new easy banking service package we could offer you. May I know if this is the right time to speak?"

The customer now understands why you are calling and might listen or schedule a good time to talk. The customer perceives the benefit that you could bring them in your call opening.

Closing a sales call

Closing a call is not the end. Closing is done to move forward towards an agenda or an objective. This is initiated when you get a closure signal in a sales meeting. So, what exactly is 'closing'?

Closing is done by 'giving commitment and taking commitment' and telling the customer what is the next thing that must be agreed upon for this agenda. Commitments from both the salesperson and the customer must be quantified and be clear to both. Only then can you say that the agenda is closed properly.

When do you close? Closing should be perfectly timed to get the best closures for a sales objective. While a sales discussion is going on, you need to listen for closure signals and decide on the right moment to close. Some common closing signals are:
- When a customer agrees with what you are saying.
- When a customer shows interest by asking more questions.
- When a customer asks you to do something.
- When a customer promises to do something.
- When a customer seems impatient.

The golden rule is: always be ready to close. Try closing, and if the customer does not agree, then revise the closure to suit both you and the customer. However, be clear that closure means both giving a commitment—saying what you will be doing next, and making sure to get a commitment—saying what you expect the customer to be doing next. In the case of the example of selling housing plans, if the customer likes a plan, the way to close would be: "I could show you a built house to give you a feel of the design. Could you spare some time tomorrow by visiting the site at 4 p.m.?"

Note here that the commitment given is 'an offer to show around the house', and the commitment taken is the customer's 'time and effort to come to the site and have a look'.

In this case, if the customer says that the site is far away, the revised closure could be: "I could alternatively come and show you a video walkthrough in my laptop. Could you spare 10 minutes for me on Wednesday, please?"

> *Closing does not mean the end of sale. It means moving ahead to the next step by giving commitments and taking commitments, which are mutually agreeable.*

In some calls, there may be opportunities for more than one 'closure'. That is, the salesperson and the customer could have agreed on more than one thing. In such cases, it is always good to sum up all the closures with the customer before ending your sales call. Remember, always try to close and move ahead when you get a closure signal. All sales calls are incomplete without proper closings.

5

How To Connect With Your Customer

We have discussed the importance of creating a rapport with your customer in the previous chapter. You build a rapport when you match the customer's way of communication by observing their body language, voice, and vocabulary and matching them with yours. This will be possible only if you succeed in making the customer talk by connecting with them and observing their style of communicating.

'Connecting' in a sales call is done to relax the customer and make them talk freely. Normally, after opening and introducing themselves, salespeople always make the mistake of starting their spiel about what they can do or how their product would be the best for the customer. Some make the mistake of firing questions to understand the customer's needs without letting the customer get comfortable with them. When you start probing the customer with a set of questions, you begin to sound like an interrogator. This is a mistake and they will soon start losing rapport with the customer.

The objective while connecting is to keep your questions as general as possible so that the customer does not feel pressurised to answer. Based on the customer's answers, you can judge how the customer likes to converse. If the customer is verbose and shares a lot of information, encourage them to talk. If the customer gives curt replies, then ask questions respectfully and in a relevant way.

So, connecting is a way of getting the customer to talk and then changing your style of communication to build a rapport with them. Rapport with your customer can be established only when you connect with them.

Connecting is always done before understanding the customer's needs or presenting product features. This is even more important when you do not know the customer very well. As we discussed, connecting is normally done by asking general questions. A universally accepted way of connecting with a known person is, "How are you?", "How's the business?", "How are you doing?", "May I help you?", or "How may I help you?"

In the case of a customer you do not know well, after opening, you could ask any general question around the 4Ps i.e., the customer's product, place, process, or people. "It is a nice facility. May I know when you started?' "Looks like a nice big office. May I know how many people work here?" Customers always feel comfortable to talk about themselves, provided the questions are not too personal or specific. Do not put the customer in the hot seat and give them a feeling of being interviewed.

From the customer's answers, you will be able to form other general questions or find topics to connect. The idea is to make the customer feel relaxed and get them to talk freely so that you can start profiling the customer and change your behaviour to suit theirs.

Let us take the example of a conversation while connecting with a customer who is buying a filing system for his office.

Salesperson	This is a nice office you have here, Sir, quite airy. And it looks big too.
Customer	Yes, it is around 30,000 square feet, and quite expensive. We would have liked to buy 35,000 square feet, but you know it is not a good investment at these high rates today.
Salesperson	30,000 square feet. What is the carpet area, Sir?
Customer	You mean how much space is there for office furniture?
Salesperson	Well, just wanted to understand if you needed any space saving furniture. We have a new range.
Customer	Sure, we would certainly be interested in that.

Salespeople could start selling their products right away by asking customers a few direct questions without connecting. But this will not allow customers to express themselves and will lead to abrupt closures.

Take a look at the conversation below to see how the salesperson's approach leads to abrupt closure:

Salesperson	What is the carpet area of the office? May I know?
Customer	You mean what area is there for office furniture?

Salesperson	Yes, we have a new furniture range which I wanted to show you. It is very well-designed and saves a lot of space.

Customer	Ok, do send an offer.

Note how in the first example of a conversation, the salesperson formulated the second general question based on the customer's first answer. This made the customer share his thoughts more openly and say that he had a space constraint.

> *Connecting is the skill of getting customers to feel comfortable in your presence and making them open up and talk freely. It is the starting point to create a rapport.*

6

How To Profile the Customer And Build a Rapport

You profile customers to build rapport so that they trust you and share their needs with you. Another reason for profiling is to close or move forward with the sales call in a more effective way.

As we discussed earlier, rapport is created by changing your communication style to match the customer's preferred style. But how they respond to it depends on their personality. Different personalities respond differently. A salesperson must be able to understand these differences and generate a good rapport.

Personality and behaviour

Personality is the combination of emotional, attitudinal, and behavioural response patterns of an individual. Behaviour is the manner of behaving or conducting oneself.

What is the difference between personality and behaviour? These words are often confused and used interchangeably.

Based on the customer's personality trait, they receive reality or information and processes them to respond in a particular way. Personality trait in an individual is developed between the ages of 3–8 years and hardly changes afterwards. It is also said that once the personality trait of a person is fixed, they cannot change it in any major way.

Behaviour can be controlled and changed to suit the people around you to a great extent. If you are soft-spoken and talk less, and you have to communicate strongly to a group to motivate them, then you have to change your behaviour to speak emphatically and influence the people in the group.

A classic example is that of a classroom where a strict teacher is present and all the children in the class are on their best behaviour. As soon as the class is over and the teacher leaves the room, all the talkative students or extroverts will start making noise and run around the room. The introvert ones will be talking softly or watching others in action.

Personality is a vast and complex science, and salespeople do not need to understand the customer's entire personality. In this chapter, you will understand the types of personality traits from a sales perspective and try and change your behaviour to match them. This will help you to build a rapport with the customer.

As shown below, there are four personality types. Based on the personality type, the customer will have certain specific traits which you must observe. These are not always visible easily, especially when the customer is in behaviour mode. People normally reveal their behaviours during interactions. They do not always project what they really are (they don't behave true to their personalities).

How To Profile the Customer And Build a Rapport 55

EXTROVERTS

INTROVERTS

Customers can be either extroverts or introverts.

For the sake of easy understanding, we can divide customers into four types of animals:

Two Extroverts—the rabbits and the puppies.
Two Introverts—the tortoises and the owls.

To generate rapport with both extroverts and introverts, you need to change your behaviour to suit them.

Now, let us look into the four different types of personalities and list some practical ways in which you can change your behaviour.

It is not easy to understand the dominant personality type of customers, as most of them would be in their behaviour modes. For example, as explained earlier, if there is a strict teacher in class, most students would be quiet. When the teacher leaves the room, the children would revert to exhibiting behaviours true to their personalities. Some would become restless and start shouting and engaging with their friends. Others who are of a different personality type would be quiet and start preparing for the next class. You have often seen your customers behave differently with you and behave differently in front of their bosses. You need to remember that although people may put on a behaviour, most people cannot control their body language and tone of voice. This is what you should try and observe keenly.

These observations need to be made when customers are not stressed and when they do not feel the need to put on an act. The best time to observe them would be at a social event.

Now, let us see what the personality traits of these four personalities are and what they show you inadvertently.

Understanding rabbits

Rabbits are extremely impatient and demanding. They are poor listeners and tend to dominate you. They are very goal-oriented and are keen to achieve what they want extremely fast. If you are not this personality type, then you need to change your behavioural style to suit them. Before you learn how to handle rabbits, you must understand their traits to know them better and profile them easily.

Personality traits	How to recognise rabbits
They are touchy and extremely sensitive. They react easily. They will also become upset and angry, often when pushed.	Will cut your sentences short. Will express strong opinions. May not listen fully to what you have to say.
They are restless and need to be doing something different all the time. They do not like being inactive.	Will not make eye contact. Will show impatience on their faces. Will not listen well. Will interrupt often.
They are aggressive in their demands, talking styles, and will try to dominate others. They want to lead.	Will demand difficult things. Will be pushy. Will be unrealistic and non-analytical when they do this.
They are active and multitasking all the time, they cannot relax at all. They need to be always engaged in some activity.	Will be engaged in many tasks. Will be selective while listening. Their hands and seated posture will show restlessness.

It is normally easy to profile rabbits as they exhibit:

- ✓ Fast rate of speech.
- ✓ Long sentences that are not structured.
- ✓ Shrill voices.
- ✓ Unstable eye contact.
- ✓ Exaggerated hand movements.
- ✓ Loud hand and body gestures.

It is prudent to observe rabbits in different situations and over several visits so that you are sure about their personality type.

Handling rabbits

Some of the behavioural changes that you need to make to build rapport with rabbits are:
- Maintain a strong eye contact, and listen actively. Rabbits like to talk and are encouraged by active listeners.
- Show an expressive and confident face expression and posture. Rabbits do not like soft people who look weak.
- Speak in short sentences and get to the point quickly.
- Show confidence when you speak by using a strong, assertive chest voice.

Closing (moving forward) with rabbits

Give them a few options and let them choose. After choosing, they tend to move ahead fast as they feel that they are in control. If you close by giving a commitment and taking theirs, they will not take their decision quickly and will skirt the decision, thinking it is your idea.

Understanding puppies

Puppies are also talkative. However, they differ from rabbits in many aspects. Puppies love to talk and listen, whereas rabbits are poor listeners. Puppies are very friendly and will make you believe that they are eating out of your hand. It is important to understand that they are like this with everybody, and that they may also be eating out of your competitor's hand. They become friendly extremely fast and tend to build personal relationships quickly. It is wise to make sure that you do not get very friendly, as they become very demanding and often put you in situations where you cannot say no.

They do not get into details and easily believe what others say. They are also poor at decision-making and depend on others to take decisions. Before you learn how to handle puppies, take a look at their typical traits which will help you to understand them better and profile them.

Personality traits	How to recognise puppies
Puppies are sociable and make friends easily. They always want to meet people and build friendly relationships.	Will be very expressive and friendly. Will talk a lot, and share their personal information and feelings.
Puppies are outgoing and quick to bond without judgment or any reservations about whom they are trying to bond with.	Will agree quickly with what you say and trust you even without thinking. Will close easily but may also retract as easily as they closed.
Puppies are talkative and very demanding about what they want.	Will quickly make demands and agree to buy very readily. Will trust everybody and seek a personal relationship.
Puppies are very lively and show it in what they do and the thoughts they express.	Face, voice, and body language will be extremely friendly, and they enjoy meeting people, but this is something that they may do with your competitors also.

It is normally easy to profile puppies as they exhibit:
- ✓ Expressive face expressions when they listen and speak.
- ✓ Friendly talk, sharing more than necessary.
- ✓ Animated hand movements and gestures.
- ✓ Modulated voices like radio jockeys.
- ✓ Ready to do things when asked.

Handling puppies

Some of the behavioural changes that you need to make to build rapport with puppies are:

- Be friendly but remember where to draw the line to say NO when required.
- Have a strong voice to say, "I know what I am saying," and project that you are dependable.
- Take more decisions for them and justify them. Build trust while taking decisions.
- Make promises that you can keep. Under promise and over deliver. Only then you can build trusty relationships with them. They will move away quickly if you let them down.
- Have energetic face expressions and listening expressions to show them that you are like them.

Closing with puppies

Give them room and take the best decision possible and say you can be trusted while closing with puppies.

Understanding tortoises

Tortoises are extremely passive and do not show any expressions. It is exceedingly difficult to understand their feelings and what they are thinking. They are also crisp and keep their conversations to the point. They are very systematic and logical in their approach. They tend to digest information and process them for their decisions. They are organised and expect others to be like them. Before you learn how to handle tortoises, take a look at their typical traits which will help you to understand them better and profile them.

Personality traits	How to recognise tortoises
Tortoises are passive and do not show what they are thinking or feeling and do not react easily.	Will not show facial expressions, but will pay attention to everything you say. Will be very observant.
Tortoises are incredibly careful about what to say, how to say or express their thoughts. Tortoises think through everything before reacting. They are slow to take decisions.	Will have slow rate of speech and take time to think through what they have to say. Will analyse what they have to say, thus leading to pauses in sentences.
Tortoises are fiercely loyal to their team, about their feelings, and what they stand for.	Will talk about processes, rules, and their present needs clearly and defend their people and their brands and choices. Are analytical in approach.
Tortoises are extremely calm in all situations and think things through before reacting or acting.	They do not react, do not show their stress outwardly, but think calmly to arrive at solutions.

Things to observe in tortoises are:
- ✓ How they keep their immediate surroundings organised and the way they dress.
- ✓ The questions they ask.
- ✓ Usage of words that are respectful without slang.
- ✓ Passive, steady posture with very few hand movements.

Note: It is a mistake to profile some people as tortoises because they talk less. It should be noted that tortoises also talk a lot, but they talk after they have built rapport, and they feel confident about trusting the person they are speaking to. However, their conversation would be structured, not rambling, and respectful.

Handling tortoises

Some of the behavioural changes you need to make to build rapport with tortoises are:
- Be well-prepared and organised in all your calls and meetings.
- Pay attention to your dressing and grooming and make sure you are smart, not loud, and not overdressed. Speak clearly, softly, and slowly. Allow tortoises to listen and process everything you say.
- Be correct and honest with what you do in front of them. Say you do not know when you do not know something. Call a spade a spade, and never exaggerate.

Closing with tortoises

Do not hastily make big commitments and take big commitments from tortoises without thinking. In fact, the best way to close with tortoises is to take incremental steps with time-bound commitments with a lot of data backing them.

Understanding owls

Owls are the 'wise people'. They are highly creative, thoughtful, honest, and rule-oriented too. They have what I call a 360-degree vision. They can see and observe things differently from others. If you look at a design and figure out how to make it work, an owl will see the same design and predict how the design will fail. However, they should not be treated as people who have a negative view of everything. If owls analyse something and accept it, then it has to be the best. Many owls love an R&D or quality control job because of this.

Owls also talk very little, but they are not structured or organised like tortoises. They go through bouts of silence when listening to others. They are also analytical, but in a creative way, unlike a tortoise. Before you learn how to handle owls, take a look at their typical traits which will help you to understand them better and profile them.

Personality traits	How to recognise owls
Owls are rigid in their beliefs, their analysis, and findings. They do not change easily.	Will resist change and not receive anything new easily.
Owls are sober and always non-reactive unless probed or encouraged to express themselves.	Will not answer questions directly. Will ask more questions and give fewer answers.
Owls are moody. Owls are highly creative but also subject to mood changes. Owls often try to find an outlet for creativity through their jokes.	Will exhibit mood changes. Will ask out-of-the-box questions, things you do not expect. Will analyse how things will fail rather than how they will work.
Owls are pessimistic and need a lot of proof to be convinced. Owls have a 360-degree analytical ability.	Will express doubts which will be sceptical.

Things to observe in owls are:
- ✓ Questions that sound like doubts.
- ✓ Pessimism.
- ✓ Resistance to change.
- ✓ Passive expressions.
- ✓ Wanting more proof.
- ✓ Long gaps between sentences.
- ✓ Repeating sentences.

Handling owls

Some of the behavioural changes you need to make to build rapport with owls and make them move forward with you are:
- Anticipate a set of questions and prepare your answers with ample proof.
- Speak slowly and confidently. Give owls time to think as they listen.
- Show empathy and understand their doubts and feelings and then give proof. Always agree with their point of view.
- Do not say anything incorrect or half-right. Owls will always remember and check afterwards.

Closing with owls

Give and take commitments only after understanding their doubts or feelings. Always ask for their opinions and understand what they feel before giving proof or closing.

Now that you have understood the four types of personalities and also learnt about the ways in which to build rapport with them, close, and move ahead, do remember that this needs to be done only with customers who are important for you, or while handling the key decision-makers, or when you are not able to make a headway. If you are able to create rapport or handle customers in the usual way without any profiling, that is perfectly fine. While practising this skill and experimenting, you may also find that many customers exhibit a bit of all four personality types. This is true as nobody is 100% a rabbit, or an owl, or a puppy, or a tortoise, but a mix of all four customer-personality types. This is why it is important for you to note down all the observations you make and focus on their dominant traits.

Sometimes, profiling can become an obsession, and you are likely to make mistakes. What is given above is a set of guidelines to start with. Only practice will make you perfect. In training interventions, I do a lot of drills to hone profiling skills. The reason you profile customers is because one rigid set of rules cannot be used to handle all types of people. People are wired differently and a good salesperson must remember this at all times.

> *Profiling is important when you face difficulties in handling certain people who are important for your business. This skill is difficult to master and takes a great deal of practice and systematic analysis over the course of many visits.*

7

How To Understand the Needs Of Your Customers

The power of information

I always stress in my training interventions that if you do not provide value benefits to the people to whom you are selling, you are not 'selling' but 'giving'. This is fine when you sell commodity products, but not value products.

Customers buy benefits and need satisfiers, and for that you must have information on customer needs. Most customers have latent needs that are dormant inside the customer, which a smart salesperson should be able to unearth. Creating needs is another important skill that a good salesperson should have.

Triggers, opportunities, and needs

As a salesperson, you would have noticed that an existing customer, with whom you have a great relationship, will express their new needs to you. The customer trusts that you will be able to satisfy them in the best way possible. This trust could be based on their experience.

A new customer will not express their needs explicitly to a salesperson who they do not know or trust enough. Most customers do not express needs till they want something badly. Even if they need something, many customers will try and find products to fit their needs by surfing the internet or asking their friends for help. For example, when the time has come to buy a new mobile phone, they tend to check out the stuff online. They might also ask a friend, whom they trust, to know more about the products which are available in the market. They will check out advertisements carefully in case they want to buy a particular brand.

The bottomline is, needs are not expressed by people in the first few visits as they do not know you well. It is also important to understand that customers need to trust you to express their needs as they think they may get conned or be made to buy something they don't need.

New customers may not express needs, but they give out ample triggers. Triggers are signals obtained from the customer where you sense an opportunity to convert the triggers to needs. For example, if you see a customer who has dandruff. So, the trigger is the dandruff, the opportunity is the cure, and as a salesperson you can unearth a need for a haircare product.

Triggers can also be expressed verbally by a customer. "I wish I could leave earlier from work." If you hear this statement being made, then you know that there is an opportunity for improving the productivity at the customer's workplace. This opportunity can translate to a filing system, where the customer can locate things easily to speed up work in his office.

A good salesperson is a keen observer and pays a lot of attention to triggers.

Let us consider a conversation between the customer and a salesperson and see what triggers can be picked up from it.

Customer	I wish we could do something about the time we spend searching for things. It's such a waste.
Salesperson	May I know why you need to search?
Customer	We need to keep some papers in the cabinet and some in bigger files outside.
Salesperson	What is the biggest size paper you need to file?
Customer	A3 paper.
Salesperson	We do have some cabinets for filing A3, A4, and A5. Would you be interested?
Customer	Well, I don't know. We bought this cabinet recently.
Salesperson	Sure, I understand. Let me work on the costs and maybe interest you with a proposal.
Customer	Ok, make sure that you study our requirements carefully.
Salesperson	Well, that is what I will do. When can I start understanding your requirements better?
Customer	Meet Phillip. You need to speak to him as he is the one who wastes maximum time searching.
Salesperson	I will meet Phillip tomorrow at 10 a.m., work out the best-sized cabinet, and evaluate the cost. I hope you will put in a word to Phillip to take some time in helping me understand this issue.
Customer	Ok.

The trigger was the customer casually mentioning the time which was wasted searching for papers. The salesperson sensed the opportunity to unearth a need for a better filing system and tried to find the best feature in his product to satisfy this need. See the above example to understand how well the salesperson closed by giving a commitment, "I'll meet Phillip tomorrow at 10 a.m. and work out the best-sized cabinet and evaluate the cost." He also took the customer's commitment, "I hope you will put in a word to Phillip to take some time in helping me understand it."

While closing, one must ensure that there are actions quantified and agreed upon by both the customer and the salesperson. Selling always involves both the customer and the salesperson moving ahead together.

> Not all customers express needs clearly, so salespeople have to catch triggers, sense opportunities, probe around these triggers, and convert them into needs.

I have often heard salespeople say that most of their customers need only good prices. If salespeople are satisfying only price needs, then they are not selling, but only giving away their products and services. Then there is no need to sell the products. You can effectively market these products on the internet and minimise your costs. Or you could easily put the products away in bargain stores with minimum price.

Understanding the needs of customers

All customers have primary and secondary needs.

The **primary need** is something that needs to be satisfied before the secondary need is addressed. For example, for a person buying a shirt the primary need may be the fit, the colour, the pattern, the drape or the design, conveniences such as pockets, and the **secondary need** may be the price.

The salesperson must think the following:

1. Will the customer buy a shirt that does not fit well just because it is 20% less costly?
2. Will the customer buy a shirt that is not designed well even if it is cheaper?
3. Will the customer buy a colour that he does not like?

You need to remember that if customers make sacrifices, it is usually around the price. In fact, a customer may pay up to 20% more for a design they like and cannot find elsewhere, or pay 10% more if the fit is better than what other similar products have to offer.

It is vital to understand the primary needs and try and satisfy these before trying to satisfy the secondary need of a customer. I know price satisfaction is important, however, primary need satisfaction is critical in order to delight buyers.

The secondary need is always the price or the budget the customer has in mind while buying. The secondary need could also be the price of the existing product that the customer is using, in which the customer is hoping to find more saving or value.

> *If you assume that the customer's need is only price, then you are treating your product as a commodity to compete with better prices. Such a product could sell on its own. When you realise that customers have multiple needs, then you are opening the first step for 'value selling'.*

Let me share a heart-wrenching story about customer needs.

A farmer had some puppies he needed to sell. He painted a sign advertising the pups and set about nailing it to a post on the edge of his yard. As he was driving the last nail into the post, he felt a tug on his overalls. He looked down into the eyes of a little boy.

"Mister," he said, "I want to buy one of your puppies."

"Well," said the farmer, as he rubbed the sweat off the back of his neck, "These puppies come from fine parents and cost a good deal of money."

The boy hung his head for a moment. Then, reaching deep into his pocket, he pulled out a handful of change and held it up to the farmer.

"I've got thirty-nine cents. Is that enough to take a look?"

"Sure," said the farmer. And with that, the farmer let out a whistle.

"Here, puppy," he called.

Out from the doghouse and down the ramp ran a dog followed by four little balls of fur. The little boy pressed his face against the chain link fence. His eyes danced with delight. As the dog and the puppies made their way to the fence, the little boy noticed something else stirring inside the doghouse. Slowly, another little ball appeared; this one was noticeably smaller. Down the ramp it slid. Then, in a somewhat awkward manner, the pup began limping towards the others, doing its best to catch up.

"I want that one," the little boy said, pointing to the limping puppy.

The farmer knelt at the boy's side and said, "Son, you don't want that puppy. He will never be able to run around and play with you like these dogs."

With that, the little boy stepped back from the fence, reached down, and began rolling up one leg of his trousers. In doing so, he revealed a steel brace running down both sides of his leg attaching itself to a specially made shoe. Looking up at the farmer, he said, "You see, Sir, I don't run well too, and he will need someone who understands."

Understanding primary needs

Customer needs can be confusing. Assuming the needs of customers leads to misunderstandings between buyers and sellers. It is necessary to first create or understand a set of primary needs and ensure that both you and the customer are clear about this.

Let us take the example of a customer who wants to buy a mobile phone.

Take a look at the set of conversations below:

Salesperson	Good morning, Sir.
Customer	I am looking for a mobile phone.
Salesperson	Which brand, Sir?
Customer	Oh! Nokia.
Salesperson	Any model you have in mind?
Customer	No... My phone broke recently.
Salesperson	Oh, I am sorry! We have these new Nokia models with Windows 10.
Customer	Ok, what is the price?

Salesperson	160 dollars, Sir, this is an incredibly special introductory offer.
Customer	I could buy a good tablet or even an iPhone for that price.
Salesperson	Sure, Sir, Windows 10 has that advantage. It uses the same platform for PC, tablet, and most office apps.
Customer	I need a phone; I already have a tablet and a laptop.
Salesperson	Nokia phones are incredibly good. It also has a warranty for one year which is international.
Customer	Why? Will it malfunction?

Now, let us analyse the conversation. The salesperson missed two triggers where he could have created needs. For the first trigger, "my phone broke recently", the salesperson could have asked (after showing some empathy) what happened. This could have led to an opportunity to create a need. The second trigger was "I need a phone; I already have a tablet and a laptop". The salesperson could have agreed and understood whether the customer was interested in any specific feature. This could have led to unearthing a need.

Let us now take the same situation and understand how it can be handled differently.

Salesperson	Good morning, Sir.
Customer	I am looking for a mobile phone.

Salesperson	We have Nokia, Apple, Samsung, LG, quite a wide range.
Customer	Ok, Nokia.
Salesperson	May I help you choose a model? Do you have any preferences?
Customer	No… My old phone broke recently.
Salesperson	Oh, I am sorry! What happened, Sir?
Customer	I dropped it from my pocket in the airport and did not realise it.
Salesperson	How did that happen? How do you carry your phone?
Customer	In my trouser's front pocket. It was a new sleek, lightweight smartphone. I could always feel my older phone if it were in my pocket. This new one was so thin and light that I did not notice it fall down, and when I realised it, it was too late.
Salesperson	I agree that thinner phones are lighter. Would you care to check out some lightweight phones which are thicker but may fit your pocket better?
Customer	I need a basic phone which is light with a good battery backup.
Salesperson	Fine, Sir, what else you do normally use?
Customer	Well, email, SMS, that is it. I do not surf much. I do not use social media. Or stream stuff…no gaming.
Salesperson	What mail systems do you use, Sir?

Customer	Well, company server mails, Gmail...and backup of some mails.
Salesperson	So you need a phone that is lightweight, has good mail handling, and storage. Let me show you three models which I think could be ok, and maybe you should also check out how they sit in your pocket.

The salesperson here was certainly tuned to understanding the customer's primary needs. He started by probing the trigger, which was how the customer lost the mobile phone, and followed it with a set of questions that gave him a good idea of the customer's primary needs, which were 'email handling', 'lightweight', and 'battery backup'. He could then shortlist 3–4 phones from his display of 5,000 odd phones, make an effort to understand more primary needs, and arrive at the best cost benefit. All customers need the best money can buy. They are most satisfied when their primary needs are satisfied.

We, as customers today, are pampered with product choices. Consider for example the mobile phone, which all of us use. We can see about 20,000 current models on the internet and 3,000 phones in each store. Since there are so many to choose from, we are confused all the time while buying products.

> *Understand primary needs of customers by probing triggers. Help customers choose products that satisfy their primary needs and then arrive at the best cost options.*

Question framing techniques

Nobody likes being probed. In fact, everybody hates being interrogated. However, a salesperson needs to ask questions to understand the customer's needs. It is not the question that irritates the customer, but the way it is asked. Let us understand some useful techniques for asking questions.

As a first rule, before you start asking questions, remember that they must be planned. Then, you need to bunch your questions up so that there is a flow of thought in the customer's mind. Let us take the example of a refrigerator. There may be several sets of questions that you may need to ask before presenting the correct model, size, capacity, shelves, cold water, freezer requirements, overall space, height, handle grip, portability, compressor type, warranty, after-sales service, location to ship, etc., to the customer. If you start firing questions randomly, customers will feel they are being interrogated. They might ask you for a form instead, promising to mail them at the earliest.

Bunching up the questions will give you a checklist of what to ask at the right time when the triggers come up.

Given below is a likely way to bunch up questions for selling refrigerators:

1. **Size and capacity-related questions**: dimensions, space, interior space, etc.
2. **Storage-related questions**: what is stored, freezer requirements, shelves, bottle storage, etc.
3. **Maintenance requirements**: power spikes, stabilisation, backup power, compressor noise, annual maintenance contract, after sales, etc.

4. **Conveniences**: cold water tap, auto defrost, auto locking door, odour control, reach, organisational convenience, etc.

When you have bunched up your questions for the products you have to sell, you will not miss questions and connect very well with triggers and needs of the customer. Questions should be asked in a conversational style, and correctly at the correct time. When you start a set of questions you could also 'request to ask'. This orients the customer's mind in thinking mode and they are more open to answer the questions.

> *Plan your questions in a structured way so that it makes it easy for customers to think through their answers.*

Given below are a set of questions framed by a salesperson.

"I would like to understand your size and space requirements to help you choose a model. Ma'am, I hope I can ask you a few questions."

"Do you have space constraints in terms of width, height, or depth in your house, Ma'am?"

"How much storage space do you need inside for vegetables?"

"What are the things you normally store?"

"How many shelves do you think will be required?"

"What do you store in your freezer, Ma'am?"

The customer is prepared to receive a set of questions related to storage, so they start to think about the same and form a mental image to answer these correctly.

Your questions should be posed as requests. This is especially important when you are dealing with the customer for the first time. The questions should also be asked respectfully like 'may I know', 'would it be possible', 'would you like', 'could you please', and 'may I ask you to' are what I would call soft phrases, as they soften the questions and make sure that the customer does not feel that they are being interrogated.

Probing techniques

You often hear about open and closed probes. An open question is asked in a way so that it does not constrain the customer's answers. Open probes are framed with—Why, When, What, Where, and How. Closed probes restrict the customer's answer to a 'yes' or a 'no', or a quantified answer. I feel both types of questions work well depending on the situation. However, I am a great fan of always making either a closed or an open probe more respectful with the phrases you have seen earlier.

More than open and closed probes, I am a great fan of using a 'positioned probe' mainly for critical questions, which I chanced upon to read about. I have tested and perfected it in many of my sales interactions with my customers as well as in my training interventions. The positioned probe is used by first asking the question respectfully, followed by giving the reason why you are asking the question, and stating the benefits to the customer.

> *Ask the question respectfully, give the reason why you are asking the question, and state the benefits to the customer.*

Let us take an example of a jeanswear store, where a well-built girl has shown up to buy a pair of jeans. The salesperson knows from experience that fit is an important need, and based on that he must lead her to the area where the products are kept. So, he asks her a seemingly harmless question, "What's your size, Ma'am?"

The customer, however, retorts by snapping, "What's your problem if I'm a large size?"

Now, if the salesperson had used a positioned probe, he would have asked, "May I know your size, Ma'am? The reason I'm asking is that we have some more sizes on display in the adjoining room, and I could lead you there if need be." When asked this way, the girl would know she was wasting her time searching there, and the answer she gave would surely benefit her. I would also emphasise here that while asking questions, respectful phrases, body language, and tone of voice are particularly important. Think through what to ask and how you are going to position them.

Take another scenario in selling, where the customer has asked you to give a quotation or an offer for a compressor. Now let us use positioned probes for the classic 'always need to know price' answer. What is your competitor supplying and at what price for the compressor capacity and specifications listed in the enquiry?

> *For critical questions, always position your questions, i.e., ask the question, give the reason for asking, and the benefits the customer will get by answering your probe.*

Here is a conversation to better understand this:

Salesperson	May I know what prices have been offered by Supreme Compressors?

Customer	Why do you want to know the competitor's price? You give us the best price possible, and we will see.

Here, the customer is pushy with the salesperson, as he fears that if the salesperson has a target price, he may sacrifice some features in the product and meet the price requirements.

An alternative way of asking this question could be:

Customer	Now that the specifications are clear, I need a price offer by tomorrow.
Salesperson	May I know the type of model and price offered by Supreme? The reason I am asking is to suggest how our product will be different and to work out cost savings.
Customer	I cannot share the exact price but I will give you an approximate price, however, please make sure you give us the most competitive price.
Salesperson	Our prices are very reasonable for the products we offer. I will work out a cost benefit for what we wish to propose. I only asked about Supreme's prices and specs to make sure you do not get an unfair offer, which cannot be compared unless I have all the facts.

It is worthwhile to note that in the above set of conversations, by positioning the questions the salesperson at least tried to ask questions in a way the customer felt like answering. Also, using the word 'reasonable' with prices helped suggest 'value' in the product instead of use of words like 'economical' or 'competitive', both of which lower the value of the product.

By using a push-selling technique and overusing feature-rich presentation, there is a risk of the customer losing interest. Many salespeople feel that if you present more and more features, you can make the customer desire the product and make them buy it. This is not always true. You do not make the customer want to buy.

You are SELLING. Not making them BUY.

Let me cite a popular anecdote regarding selling.

A young salesperson had lost an important sale. He was terribly upset.

When speaking about this to his sales manager the young salesperson shrugged. "I guess," he said. "It just proves that you can lead a horse to the water, but you cannot make it drink."

"Son," said the sales manager. "Let me give you a piece of advice. Your job is not to make it drink. It's to make it thirsty."

—Toast Finder

> *In the post-Covid age, consumers no longer have wants or desires. In fact, their needs also have been relegated to life simplifiers. Only trusted relationships will sell.*
>
> *Also, creating needs will first require building trust.*

The main premise of Simon Sinek's bestselling book, *Start With Why*, can be summarised in his statement, "People don't buy what you do; they buy why you do it."

It should make sense, in that case, for customers to know you well enough to trust you. And then feel that they need you and your products and your services.

8

VALUE SELL TO CUSTOMERS

What is a commodity product and what is a value product?

This question haunts most sales and marketing people. Commodity products, such as milk, gold, and gas, are easily available to buy, and their prices as well as their features are standardised. That means that at all points where they are dispensed in their basic form, the prices are standard. The prices may go up or down depending on demand and supply, but generally, they remain the same at a given point of time. Regional prices may vary a bit, depending on their taxes and freight. The source price, however, is standard. There are various bodies that regularise the prices of these products, but generally supply/demand and market consumerism control the prices.

As we know, the needs for commodities are a given. Most of the customers understand these needs and buying decisions are taken based on price and location. For example, if you are buying milk, you know the prices are standard everywhere. So, a decision around where to buy it from or from whom is taken depending on the brand you trust and your convenience. Some might buy it from the supermarket, some from a nearby store, while others might get it delivered to their homes or go to a farm and buy it.

Who makes money selling a commodity product? The person who produces it, or the one who sells it, or the middlemen? Well, nobody. If there is a shortage and the prices go up, the middlemen make more money. But soon enough, the supply gap gets filled, and it is business as usual. While a customer buys a commodity product purely on the basis of price, a value product is sold on the basis of needs of the customer. The value addition in the product must be enough to demand higher prices and margins.

Instead of selling potatoes which a farmer has been growing, if he decides to add value by selling cut potatoes or mashed potatoes to cater to the demands of the chips and the curry market then they are value adding. The need for fat-free milk, de-starched potatoes, or cut potatoes will create a value that is more than that of the commodity product and get him better prices and a greater margin.

For example, if the farmer stops selling potatoes and starts selling de-starched potatoes, he shifts the need of the customer from potatoes to health. The value is now enhanced. From selling a commodity like potatoes and fighting prices in a crowded market, the value becomes healthy potatoes for which better prices can be obtained and more value can be delivered to customers.

> *If a potato costs 10c per pound after farming and retails at 30c per pound as a potato, it is value added to at least $1 per pound when it turns into chips or fries.*
>
> *Also, creating needs will first require building trust.*

You have understood by now that selling is all about satisfying the needs of the customer and building a relationship with them along the way. Once you have understood—both the primary and the secondary needs, you have to find products that cater to them.

What is mutual benefit? It should benefit customers to buy when the products satisfy needs effectively. Sellers should also benefit by getting a good price. If buyers and sellers are not benefitted mutually, this process is not selling, it is merely giving. To take this thought to its logical conclusion, a salesperson is adding value only when they are selling and not giving, or, for want of a better word, supplying.

Do customers buy products? Most customers do not buy products, or, as we discussed before, they buy brands. There are buying benefits or trust from the products or brands. There are too many products to choose from, and hence, customers are confused. How a salesperson finds a fit between needs and product benefits is the value addition made in sales.

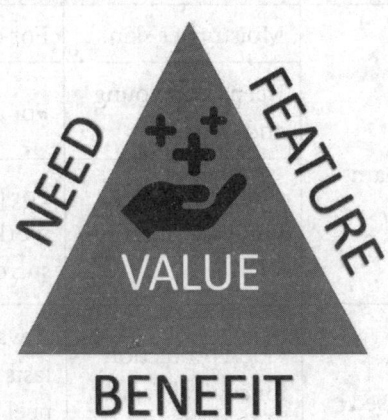

What is 'value selling'? It is explained clearly in the visual shown above.

The salesperson must find the right product features to match the customer's needs. These features should translate to benefits which could be quantified. The fit between needs, features, and benefits is what the customer perceives as a value to make a buying decision. This can be represented in the triangle above. There may be many needs unearthed while understanding the customer's requirements. All these needs have to be summarised and represented in such a way so that products can be shortlisted effectively.

> *Customers buy benefits and remember the features of the products if their needs are well satisfied.*

Different need-feature-benefit examples are mapped below for a few products:

Features	Benefits	Needs
Aloe vera enriched cream.	Moisturises skin.	For dry skin.
	Keeps skin young and fresh.	For ageing skin.
	Prevents irritation.	For people who work in harsh surroundings.
Polyester-based paint with teflon.	Good protection for several years.	A wall paint that lasts and does not peel off.
	Better water and stain resistance.	To avoid spillages and stains.

Lubricant with sludge busters.	Good pickup.	For driving in heavy traffic.
	Engine does not stall.	When gears need to be changed frequently.
Surgical stainless steel cases in watches.	Does not rust.	For a watch that can withstand the wear and tear of regular use.
	Long-lasting.	
	Does not cause skin allergies.	When there is a case of metal allergy.
Cellulose acetate plastic frames in eyewear.	Environment-friendly.	For spectacles that do not irritate the skin.
	Skin-friendly.	
	Soft on skin.	
Polycarbonate lenses sunglasses.	Lightweight.	Sunglasses for outdoor activities.
	Shatter-resistant.	
	100% UV protection.	
Mercerised fabrics.	Retains colours and richness.	When rich colours are required that do not fade fast.
	Lasts for 40 washes without fading.	

2 ply, heat-set, fine-count yarns in fabrics.	Lasts long.	When a fabric is required for a uniform.
	Shines more.	For a richer look.
	Drapes well.	For a good fit.

A salesperson who arrives at an understanding of the customer's primary needs would be able to fit a 'value statement' if need-feature-benefit are clear. For example, while making a presentation of a value statement for a special range of sunglasses, you could say, "Sir, you said you travel extensively and do a lot of field work. May I suggest polycarbonate sunglasses? These will give you 100% UV protection. Since you also said you ride a bike and are frequently on construction sites, the polycarbonate one is better, as it is shatter resistant. It will protect your eyes."

This way you have covered several needs of the customer. One was exposure to sunlight, and the others were the risk of falling objects in a construction site, the glasses falling down while riding a bike, and the risk of accidents.

Customers finally buy your products or services if they perceive a 'value' which is better than what they have seen in other products or services. By allowing customers to choose products based only on the price, and not understanding the value, you risk making your products mere commodities. Today, just value selling is not enough to keep customers happy and to build lasting relationships. Value selling is only the start of a healthy customer relationship. What you need to develop is the power to sell and keep the sale mutually beneficial.

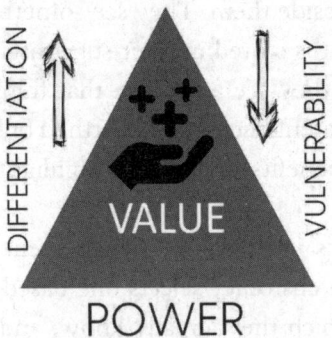

When there is a closed loop of need, feature, and benefit, there is value in a sales call.

If the value offered by you is high and different from what others can offer, then there is a 'differentiation', which increases the value and improves 'power' in the relationship. Why should there be a differentiation? If there is a differentiation, other products cannot compete with the proposed value of your products. If there are many products that offer the same value, you should be constantly improving products to provide better value. By increasing the value, you are reducing the vulnerability.

> *The more the differentiation, the less the vulnerability and the more the 'power' in the relationship.*

Storytelling value—addressing latent needs

Storytelling is one of the most important skills used to build value around a brand and its latent needs and benefits. What are latent needs and benefits? It is important to understand these. Latent needs are unearthed by salespeople as they are often not expressed by customers. Many customers have needs that are buried inside them. They see something they like and forget about it. It is stored in their subconscious mind. Then, suddenly, when they see a product that fulfils the need, they want to buy it. Latent needs are unearthed only if a salesperson presents more benefits and subtly highlights what is called 'hero features'.

Hero features in products trigger latent needs. A watch is just a watch; a customer selects one based on its looks and basic features which they already know, and then somebody tells them that it can monitor their heart rate and oxygen levels. These sets of hero features trigger a latent need in the customer. The customer may have heard about someone who died of a heart attack due to over-exercising. The feature of the watch would trigger a latent need which was buried deep in a customer's subconscious mind. It will suddenly make them want that particular watch. And they may end up buying it. If you elaborated on the value by explaining how the feature worked and told the customer about its benefits, it would accelerate the buying urge in them.

So, hero features stand out and lend themselves to storytelling.

Let us compare the way the car Nano was sold, and the way Alto, with power steering was sold. Nano was one of the lowest-priced cars in the world and was touted as a poor man's car in India. All Indians, it was believed, aspire to own a car. This brand aimed to meet the aspirations of millions of Indians who rode cycles and two-wheelers and used a gruelling and overcrowded public transport system. It has always been unsafe to ride a two-wheeler in India where the roads are packed with vehicles and pedestrians. Nano is also said to have targeted women drivers in particular. The car was priced at under Rs 2,00,000 or under $2,500.

Despite all calculations, it did not do well in India. It met all the primary needs such as good fuel economy, aesthetics, and low maintenance costs. That was what marketers in India were confident about. There was great anticipation before it was launched. Former First Lady of the United States Michelle Obama wanted to see it and check it out. In fact, she did.

I also loved its looks. My prediction was that it would be a game changer. My belief was that it would replace the popular autorickshaws (tuk-tuks) because it was a safer mode of transport.

Nano was a basic vehicle with no power steering, no air conditioning, and no safety features worth mentioning.

Then, along came Alto, presenting a hero feature—or so they claimed. At that time, only the expensive cars came with this feature. The company made an advertisement featuring a celebrity driving an Alto in a crowded street in India. It showed viewers what a nightmare it was to drive a car in India, squeezing it into narrow spaces, constantly twisting and turning the steering wheel, and brushing past other cars on traffic-clogged roads with inches to spare.

In this advertisement, the celebrity expertly navigated through traffic with one hand. In fact, he even drove on the pavement and came back on to the road to join the stream of traffic. This 30-second clip triggered the customer's latent need to drive across traffic-clogged roads with an easy-to-navigate and sensitive steering system. Many customers in India, yearned for this.

In my opinion, this dealt a death blow to all cheap cars, including Nano. The cheaper cars tried to add the feature since customers wanted them, but clearly, Alto had ignited the aspiration.

I am tempted here to digress and discuss another favourite topic of mine called 'hero feature leadership'. If a brand brings in a differentiated feature or a hero feature, then it leads the market with this feature. Soon, there will be followers who would simply copy the feature. Others would find ways to get around patents, add similar features, and sell products by enhancing their value. I call them challengers. The brand that put in the feature first is the leader.

What happens next? The leader coolly reduces the price to keep increasing the market share. The challenger goes ahead by reducing the price further. The leader continues to lead, but does the challenger continue to challenge? No. The challenger becomes a follower. This is because the challenger tried to disrupt the leader with the price. The challenger did not address the latent need better. It will be hailed as a challenger only if it brought in better features to fit the latent need rather than the price. By following a me-too approach, the challenger ends up being a follower.

> *Hero features trigger latent need in customers. They stand out when they lend themselves to storytelling. Remember, creating needs will first require building trust.*

Salespeople constantly need to be aware of the latent needs of customers. They can do this only if they have a set of hero features and stories that revolve around the features of their products.

Storytelling is another important skill that salespeople need to cultivate in order to build value around their products.

The most expensive watch sold in the world was sold for $5 million. What did it have? No gold, no diamonds, and no precious stones—in fact, nothing of perceived value. What made a buyer invest in it? The watch was made of steel. That too, not even stainless steel. This meant that it would rust eventually. So, what prompted the buyer to purchase it?

This watch was not made by a famous brand, or even a famous watchmaker. What he did was simple, but different. He assembled the watch with mechanical moving parts—at least 200 of them or so. All these were handcrafted and correctly fitted and assembled. What became the clincher ultimately was that he made it out of a special kind of steel. This steel was obtained after he dived into the sea and salvaged it from the doomed *Titanic*, making several trips underwater to forage for scraps from the sunken ship. The watch was created to mark the 100th anniversary of the glorious *Titanic*. What a valiant effort and what a story!

This story would have been incomplete if the salesperson had not told it in the correct way with the right amount of passion required for sharing it with customers.

The second-most expensive watch was sold for $4 million. It was also handcrafted, had many moving parts, and took a great deal of effort to put it together. The clincher was the story. The alarm chimes of the watch matched the Lourdes church bells in France. It was a mammoth task and the maker needed two years to complete it. The 'effort story' was sold as a watch for $4 million.

Luxury products that spark aspirations need a story for buyers to find value in them. The aspirational need is strongly driven by a 'story flaunt value'.

Let us take the case of a non-luxury product. Here is an interesting anecdote:

A lady was browsing in a store when she noticed some fridge magnets that were being sold as souvenirs. Some were very intricate and expensive, while the others were cheap. She then picked up a magnet that looked cheaply-made. It was a square piece of wood with a little magnet glued to its back. On the front, there was a symbol painted in red, which looked like an eight-pointed star drawn by a child.

"What is this?" she asked the salesperson.

"Ah, this is a magic symbol for Icelandic fishermen!" said the salesperson.

The salesperson went on to add that when Iceland was first occupied by the Vikings, most people's livelihoods depended on fishing. It was a dangerous occupation given the harsh climate. The Vikings worshipped the Norse gods, and this star was the magic symbol the fishermen wore or carved on their boats to appease the gods and bring good fortune and provide protection for their fishing trips.

"How much is it?" the lady asked.

"10 euros," said the salesperson.

The lady bought five of them.

> *Products especially luxury ones, need a story for buyers to find value in them. The aspirational need is strongly driven by a 'story flaunt value'.*

We have all heard that today's empowered buyers are 60% of the way through a buying cycle by the time they meet a salesperson because they have researched about the product online. But if this self-serve model works so well, then why do they always doubt whether they are buying the right product. They always feel there is something better. They try and research the net or from known sources a lot before they meet sales people these days. Their impressions around what they want are already formed by the time the sales person gets involved. That is why when the sales person tries to understand the needs the minds are confused.

Around 60–70% of enterprise sales opportunities end with the buyer deciding to live with the status quo? Why would a buyer waste all that time and effort only to do nothing?

Customers normally lack the time and expertise to make the right buying decision. Due to urgency of buying, buyers and sellers dumb everything down to where all offerings become commoditised, so the only differentiator is price. Unfortunately, what they find is that the dumbed-down version does not solve a problem or really meet their need, so they stick with the status quo or buy the cheapest suboptimal solution.

When I fall sick, the night before I visit the doctor, I go online to figure out what is troubling me. So, by the time I show up at the doctor's office, I am just looking for him to write me a prescription. I just need the doctor to enhance my incomplete buying vision so that it closely represents what I need.

Admittedly, for commoditised products, buyers can buy online because they meet a basic need, but for complex needs, the salesperson "must shine the light of insight on the buyer's confusing buying vision so that they can fully appreciate the value of your product," says Michael Harris, well-known author and CEO, Insight Demand.

A Gartner survey indicates that 74% of buyers felt salespeople spend too much time talking about their products without providing a story or trying to connect to their customer's needs. Finally, salespeople leave it up to customers to figure out why they should buy their product. This product strategy is not successful because only 34% of buyers felt salespeople could articulate value. If salespeople want to sell value, they should establish a clear connect between the product features and benefits to the customer's needs.

9

HOW TO SELL TO DECISION-MAKERS

A sanitary napkin brand was reviewing sales per region and they found that sales were the highest in a small, less-populated state. States with 10 times its population sold half of what they sold. The marketing team was curious and so they sent their executive to that state to find out. Their research substantiated the need for thick and more absorbent pads. Women needed these especially if they had to work all day.

Off went the marketing person to meet some customers. He started by sitting down on a bench in front of a retail store that sold his brand's pads. Eager to understand customers, he waited all day, but he did not find any women shopping here. About 20 men had come and gone during the day and all of them bought something at the store.

Finally, he approached the shopkeeper and asked, "Didn't you sell any pads today?"

"Yes," said the shopkeeper. "Didn't you see? Around 20 pads were sold. I am doing very well."

"But," said the puzzled marketing person, "I saw only men buying things. I couldn't make out what they were carrying in their bags."

"Yes, they were carrying pads. All of them bought pads. Some buy pads every week," said the shopkeeper.

"Wow! Women don't shop for their pads themselves?" The marketing person was confused. "Don't they like the product? Are they asking for any improvements?"

"People like the product, but it will be better if they are made thinner," said the shopkeeper who was eager to sell more. "Make it as thin as possible. Even half the thickness of what you are giving now will be good."

The executive was stumped. Everywhere people asked for thicker pads, but this place was the opposite. He could not figure out why this was so, but he wanted to use this opportunity to understand the customer's need. Respectfully, he stated that normally women preferred the pads to be thicker. Why did they want them to be thinner in this place?

The shopkeeper said a bit apologetically, "Sir, this is a hot place. Very humid and sweaty. So, the men here use these pads on a daily basis. You see, we wear only white shirts here and sweat shows very quickly on them. So, most men wear these pads between their neck and collar. The pads absorb sweat very well and keep the shirts less stained. But the pads are too thick, so many users are unhappy. We can increase the sales by at least two times if we make them thinner."

The marketing person went back to his office wiser and smarter.

The needs of markets and their customers are different. They are driven by practices and by how products are used.

It is no wonder that when double-bowl washing machines were first launched, the state of Punjab in India clocked the highest sale. Even now, these washing machines sell very well there. However, people there were not using the machines to wash clothes. They used them to make a popular beverage called lassi, which is consumed in very large quantities by people in Punjab.

Salespeople spend enormous amounts of time in trying to sell the values of their products. Unfortunately, they hit roadblocks whenever the buyer feigns interest (and sometimes even agrees to the value propositions), but finally backs off from buying.

They have many reasons to cite:
- I do like it, but the price seems too high.
- Give it to me for free and I will try it. If it works, I will take it.
- Give me some time, I cannot decide.

Some of these blocks could be an objection or a concern. An objection is an interest shown by buyers. It is normally raised by buyers while hoping to be convinced that they are taking the right decision forward. These are also called buying signals. Buying signals are a good thing. A salesperson could handle the objection correctly and end up convincing the customer. However, this requires knowledge of the right way of handling the customer. This is addressed in the next chapter.

Getting a stall while selling is different from running into a sales objection. When a customer agrees with the point of view but does not move ahead, there could be many reasons for such a pause. In his book, *New Conceptual Selling*, Stephen Heinemann says there could be basic issues to deal with here. Here is an example of how crucial decisions are made on the basis of a basic issue. An old lady was having trouble buying a phone. She was convinced about all the features of a phone which she had selected. It had good audio reception (a primary need for her), a good camera she badly wanted, and a large display which suited her shortsightedness. Still, she ended up buying a phone which did not have a good camera and sharper display. She chose a phone that had a better grip so it would not slip out of her hands (something the salesperson realised later). She had a bad experience with her previous phones that she had dropped and broken. This need was never understood or brought out in her interactions. She had not bothered to reveal it as she had felt embarrassed. For her, the grip was an important need and a basic issue.

However, the first step to better understanding whether there are basic issues is that the salesperson could be presenting value to a person who is not a decision-maker. Only a person who is a decision-maker would appreciate the value and benefits in a higher priced product or service.

It is often assumed that the decision-maker is the most powerful person in the organisation who is buying, or the most powerful person in the family or group who is shopping at a retail store. Sometimes, it is assumed that the most knowledgeable person is the decision-maker. They have the expertise to take the decision. But this may not be always the case. If so, who is a decision-maker? How do you find decision-makers?

Before understanding who is a decision-maker, it is necessary to understand what kinds of people engage themselves in a buying decision, or who a salesperson addresses while selling. There are four types of customers you will encounter in the selling process.

1. **Gatekeepers**: Normally, these are the first ones to connect and deal with salespeople.
2. **Decision-makers**: These are the people who prefer to remain in the background and let gatekeepers handle sales meetings. They present themselves only if they are needed by gatekeepers. However, they are often consulted without the salespeople being aware of it. A filtered set of information reaches the decision-makers.

But these are the people who have the responsibility of deciding to buy the product.
3. **Influencers**: These people are the ones decision-makers depend on to take decisions. The decision-makers trust influencers for their knowledge and expertise and normally do not get directly involved in evaluations.
4. **Opinion leaders**: These are people outside the sphere of influence of decision-makers. They come into play only if decision-makers cannot decide or the decision about buying is out of their scope, too big, or complicated.

Salespeople are pushed into a corner, often requiring to reduce the price by customers who want to fog their actual needs. This smokescreen forces salespeople to either reduce their prices and value, or walk away from the sale.

Gatekeepers have only two needs—lowest possible price and fastest shipping. They try their best to reduce the value in the products offered and commoditise them. Salespeople have to recognise the objection raised by the buyer to sell value and find out who the decision-makers are and who the influencers are.

Decision-makers are always keen to discuss their primary needs first before they discuss the price. For example, while buying a shirt the basic issue is the fit. Only a decision-maker, that is, the person who is going to wear the shirt can decide if the fit is right. The price, colour, and print are secondary. Identifying a decision-maker and understanding their needs is important. In industrial products, quality standards, features, safety, and service can become primary needs over the price. These needs are mostly highlighted as important by decision-makers. Commercial people like purchase people and buyers in an organisation would normally express their primary needs as the price.

Summarised in four quadrants are traits of four types of people in an organisation.

Decision-makers	Gatekeepers
Responsible for product usage	Responsible for bringing down prices
Responsible for product failure	Try to 'commoditise' product
Have the 'decision power' to change	Prefer to have many suppliers
Influencers	**Opinion leaders**
Have the trust of decision-makers	Are only consulted
Have more information	Have no primary responsibility
Can influence decision-makers	Can be a source of information

So, how do you know who is the decision-maker? It is quite simple. First, you must ascertain that the person you are dealing with is the gatekeeper. If the assumed gatekeeper is willing to listen and understand 'value', they could be a decision-maker. If they do not, then the salesperson pushes the assumed decision-maker to either use the product which has higher value by trying it or pushes to change their existing product. If the assumed decision-maker resists change or usage, then the person is not a decision-maker, but a gatekeeper.

Your next step would be to request a meeting with the person to whom they can make a sales pitch. Forcing the presumed gatekeeper to decide about value is the best way to ascertain whether they are the actual gatekeeper.

The decision-maker could see value and maybe bring in opinion leaders or influencers to work with salespeople. From then on, the tunnel to value sell becomes larger and wider. A deeper understanding evolves. More doors are opened. Stronger relationships can be developed with the organisation in this way.

Remember, at no point in this process should a gatekeeper feel that they are being left out. A good salesperson maintains smooth relationships with all the people in the organisation they are selling to.

It is also important to build all-round relationships with many people in an organisation. Frequently, salespersons build relationships with the buyer alone, and this leads to a degree of vulnerability. What if the person leaves the organisation or is transferred or starts disliking the salesperson? It is best to build bonds with more than one person, keeping these possibilities in mind.

Even in the case of group buying, you will often see that when a house or a car is being bought, the whole family will be involved in the process. Here, it is wise to pay attention to all the people. Look for cues, find out who the decision-maker is, and ascertain the sell value.

10

How To Handle Customer Concerns

What are customer concerns? These are doubts expressed by the customers while buying. Why do people have doubts? Doubts arise because people want to be absolutely sure of what they are buying. Many salespeople hate it when customers object to something or have doubts. Customer sales objections or concerns crop up only when customers want to buy a product. If customers were not interested in what the salesperson was presenting, surely, they would not have concerns. They would simply say, "Can you show me something else?"

Hence, customer objections, concerns, or doubts are strong buying signals. When customers have doubts, they are sending an invitation to the salesperson saying, "Come and convince me that I am taking the correct decision." In fact, it is particularly good to invite objections/concerns/doubts from the customer and use the correct method to convince them. They would then be happy about having made the right decision.

Let us see how best you can handle these concerns.

Handling product concerns

Product concerns when raised by a customer are a sure indication that they are interested in a product. Often, many salespeople cannot distinguish between a genuine question about the product and a doubt about it. A question is raised by customers in order to get information. A doubt is expressed when they feel the need to be convinced. When customers ask questions, they need only answers, not convincing.

The box below presents ways in which customers express themselves while buying a cupboard.

Questions	Concerns/Doubts
How many shelves are there in the cupboard?	Will the number of shelves be enough?
How strong are the shelves?	Are the shelves strong enough to take the weight?
What is the material used here…wood?	You are using wood for the shelves! Is it ok?
What is the price?	Why is the price so high?
Is it long-lasting?	I am not sure it will last long.

When a customer has a concern or a doubt, the first step in handling it correctly is to understand the doubt or concern, agree that they are right in expressing so, articulate clearly that you understand, and then address their concern. This makes the customer feel important and more open to accepting of the explanation that the salesperson has to offer.

In short,
1. Understand the customer's concern fully.
2. Agree with the customer's concern or say that you understand the concern.

3. Give reliable reassurance about the concern.

Customer	I sense that the shelves may not be strong.
Salesperson	Ma'am, they are extraordinarily strong and made of CRS powder-coated steel.
Customer	Ok, but they are so thin that they do not look strong enough.
Salesperson	A small boy can sit on it, Ma'am. Nothing will happen.
Customer	Well, there is nobody here to check, so I guess I will see some more designs.
Salesperson	Sure, Ma'am, we have many more designs.

What happened in this kind of handling of a concern is that the customer did not trust the salesperson. If a concern is not handled properly, customers end up having more concerns.

Let us look at an alternative way of handling the above-mentioned concern.

Customer	I sense that the shelves may not be strong.
Salesperson	The shelves are made of CRC powder-coated steel. May I understand why you feel that they may not be strong?
Customer	Well, the books I have are hardbound and very heavy.
Salesperson	How many books would you be storing, Ma'am? I want to be sure of the weight of the books on the rack.

Customer	Well, at least 10 books.
Salesperson	I understand, Ma'am. And certainly the books will be heavy, but 10 books will not be heavy enough to bend the shelves, Ma'am. They are made of steel and quite strong. I will however double-check in the evening and confirm.
Customer	Otherwise, I quite like the design, the colour, and the compactness.
Salesperson	May I then take an order for the cupboard with a 20% advance? I'll surely confirm whether it can take 10 hardbound books. Would that be ok?
Customer	Ok.

In this conversation, the customer wanted to be sure that the shelves could take the weight of books. The salesperson understood the customer's concern. He probed further to understand the doubt clearly by positioning the questions correctly. He then accepted the customer's concern as important and reassured the customer that he would double-check, confirm, and get back. All this added up and the customer was convinced.

> *Pay proper attention to the customer's product-related concerns, understand them fully, agree with the customer's point of view, and justify with proof, or offer to double check and revert to the customer.*

Handling price concerns

Price concerns are also buying signals in the sense that they show the customer is interested in the product. The customer only wants to be sure that they are paying the correct price. The customer may also be mentally comparing cheaper products with this one.

The method of handling price concerns is also the same:

1. Understand the concern. Does the customer feel the price is high in general or are they comparing it with another product? If the customer is comparing with another product, understand that product clearly.
2. Agree by saying, "I understand". This will help the customer be sure that you are not confronting their perception.
3. Justify the price by listing the features and benefits of your products and how they are different from what it is being compared with. Also discuss what features are unique to your product to warrant a different price than the one it is being compared with.

It is especially important for salespeople to understand what their competitors are offering and the differences, if any, from their product. You must know, respect, and understand your competitors.

Let us take two types of sales conversations regarding a sale of a popular brand's tablet and spot the difference.

Customer	What is the price of the 7 inch?
Salesperson	225 dollars, Sir.

Customer	225 dollars seems a bit steep.
Salesperson	Sir, this is a tablet of a big brand. It is much better than the cheaper ones. Those are Chinese products.
Customer	How can it be? It seems to have the same features.
Salesperson	Yes, Sir, but this is not Chinese. Our brand is Korean.
Customer	So, are the prices decided based on the country of origin?
Salesperson	No, Sir, but the unbranded ones are cheaper.
Customer	So, I must pay extra for the branded ones?
Salesperson	Sure, Sir, a good brand assures better quality.
Customer	Well, I don't understand how.
Salesperson	We offer warranty for one year as the quality is better.
Customer	Warranty means I am likely to have a problem.
Salesperson	No, Sir, it is like insurance.

Observe here that when the customer raised a price concern, the salesperson moved into the justifying mode as he felt that he was going to lose the customer based on the price. In such a scenario, most salespersons panic and start justifying the price without any basis. When the customer does not become convinced, arguments start. A passionate salesperson will defend their product to the hilt but will end up losing the customer's trust. Salespeople should understand that customers who raise price concerns want to buy. The bottomline is that they are interested in the product. They just want to be sure that they are paying the correct price.

Let us now look at a different conversation:

Customer	What is the price for the 7 inch?
Salesperson	225 dollars, Sir.
Customer	That seems a bit steep.
Salesperson	This is a popular brand, with Windows 10 and two USB-C ports. May I understand why you feel the price is high?
Customer	Yes, I saw the same OS, same USB ports, and hardware being sold cheaper. Only the brand was different.
Salesperson	May I know the brand you are comparing it to, Sir?
Customer	The brand is Smart Tab Genie. I don't know more details.
Salesperson	I understand, Sir, I too am not aware of such a product. It may be good. But allow me to explain certain quality tests and design features in our product that are different.
Customer	Still, the price difference is huge.
Salesperson	How much is the price difference, Sir?
Customer	About 50 dollars.

Salesperson	I understand, Sir, let me explain what you get for 50 dollars more.
Customer	Fine, are you sure this is the best price you can offer?
Salesperson	Yes, Sir, I am sorry we are not able to give you a better price.
Customer	Ok, I will take it.

Here the salesperson tried to understand the price concern, understood the features being compared, and also grasped the comparison regarding the price, and reassured the customer about the quality with quantified benefits. He made sure that he was not criticising his competitors. Good salespeople respect their competitors, but love their own products.

Quantified benefits are better than general statements in sales.

Who is going to buy a product from a salesperson who says, "This brand is good" or "This product is good?"

People are interested in quantified benefits: "We make products that have undergone 32 quality checks." "We have over 200 design patents." "20% of our product portfolio comprises of new products." "We support you in 120 countries." "We have a 24/7 door service."

All salespeople need to write down at least 25 brand benefits with differentiators before they start selling. This needs to be done because we are living in an era where customers are acutely aware of price concerns, and need reinforcement regarding brands and their product features and benefits.

Handling after-sales service concerns

After-sales service concerns arise when customers want long-lasting products. They would like to ensure that there is enough service backup for the products they buy.

What exactly is service? You will hear many salespeople say, "Our service is good." Such general statements have no meaning as far as customers are concerned.

Service expectations from customers could be the following:

- Is the product serviceable?
- Will there be spares available? If so, for how many years?
- Will it become outdated or change designs often?
- Where do I get replacement parts?

Is there a warranty? Is it national or international? A warranty ensures the product is fixed in case there is a problem during the warranty period. A guarantee ensures that the product is replaced during the guarantee period.

- What care should be taken while using the product?

Salespeople selling durables often use their service differentiators to sell their products. Many service differentiators are important from the customer's point of view. However, be wary of going overboard.

Take a look at the following statement of overcommitment in service:

"We have 3,000 service centres in our country alone"—the way a customer could perceive this is: Will there be that many problems? Isn't your product service free?

"We have a lifetime warranty"—the way the customer could perceive this is: Is it the product's lifetime or my lifetime?

"We guarantee performance for three years"—the way the customer could perceive this is: Would you be repairing the product if there is a problem or would you be replacing the product?

Most service concerns arise from the customer's poor understanding of what you are offering as a service backup. Salespeople also overstate their service differentiators to sell products. The 'conditions apply' asterisk creates confusion and mistrust. So, customers are uncertain about what service they are getting as nobody has the time to read service manuals and understand what is written in small print. It is critical for salespeople to be transparent when they talk about their service backup.

Let us see how best to handle service-related concerns.

The framework for handling service concerns is the same as that of product or price handling. First, understand the concern and need for service, accept the customer's point of view by saying that in an extreme case problems could arise, and reassure the customer with what you can service. Do not overstate service capability.

To sum up, the method of handling a service concern correctly is:

1. Understand the concern fully and seriously.
2. Accept that problems may occur very rarely—do not say 'during misuse'.
3. Reassure by explicitly stating the service you can provide.

Let us take two sets of sales conversations and see the difference.

Customer	Is there a guarantee?
Salesperson	Yes, Sir, we provide one-year warranty.
Customer	So, if there is a problem, will I get a replacement?
Salesperson	Either a replacement or we will rectify the defect, provided it falls within the terms.
Customer	What are the terms?
Salesperson	We will be giving you a warranty book. Everything is mentioned in it, Sir, in 14 languages.
Customer	I will hold you responsible if there is a problem.
Salesperson	No problem, Sir, we are always here. This is our number. Just call us.
Customer	Is this your number or a call centre's?
Salesperson	It is a 24/7 call centre. They will pass the message to the service people.
Customer	Great! So, service is not your problem.
Salesperson	We only sell. We are authorised distributors. Service is provided by the brand. From the company.
Customer	So, do I have to deal with two different agencies?
Salesperson	We are all one and the same. Only the organisations are different.
Customer	Fine. I will get back to you soon.

In this scenario, the customer started suspecting the salesperson. Where did the salesperson begin to lose the customer? The concern was that if there was a product problem, would the customer get a replacement? The answer was not clear to the customer. Notice that the salesperson backed away from servicing, indicating very clearly that service was not his problem. The customer was in no way assured regarding the concern and so he stepped back.

Let us look at a different scenario:

Customer	Is there a guarantee for the pump?
Salesperson	Certainly, Sir, we provide one-year warranty for the electrical motor and pump running. External damages, I am sorry to say, are not covered in the warranty, Sir.
Customer	So, if there is a problem, I will get a replacement, will I?
Salesperson	I am sorry, Sir. We may not replace the pump unless it is unused as there will be wear and tear. We will rectify the pump free of cost at your doorstep.
Customer	That is what all salespeople say when it comes to service. Later, you will wash your hands off it.
Salesperson	Why do you feel that way, Sir? We are a reputed brand and have been selling and servicing pumps for 25 years.
Customer	Earlier, all products had good backup. Now, with stressed margins, nobody wants to provide service.

Salesperson	I understand your concern, Sir. We have a 24/7 support centre which you can call, and we service within 48 hours in the top 16 towns. These towns are listed here.
Customer	So, you will only sell and not service?
Salesperson	You could also call us, Sir. However, we have a separate, competent team for servicing. This is because they are well equipped to deal with breakdowns.
Customer	I will only hold you responsible.
Salesperson	This is my number, Sir. There won't be any problem. In case you need assistance, do call us, Sir. We always like to keep in touch with our customers.
Customer	Thanks.
Salesperson	So, can I bill this pump, Sir?
Customer	Yes.

This is a stark contrast to the previous example. Here, the salesperson showed genuine interest in the customer's concern, tried to understand the nature of the concern, and reassured the customer without any false promises. All customers respect you when you are transparent regarding what you can do and feel sorry about what you cannot. Transparency is the key to building trust.

Handling scepticism

Customers are usually sceptical about a product or service because of a bad experience. They raise doubts when they have bought similar products that did not meet their expectations, experienced service delays, and lost their trust because of bad sales or service experience. You now know that you must handle doubts by first understanding the doubt, empathising, or agreeing with the customer's point of view and giving reassurance or proof. Sometimes, customers do not agree even when you handle their doubts correctly. This is when you must realise that the customer has had a bad experience and hence, has become sceptical.

The right method of handling scepticism is given below:

1. Understand the doubt.
2. Agree about the viewpoint to avoid an argument.
3. Reassure.

If the customer shows concern again:

1. Check if the customer has had a bad experience before.
2. Understand the experience and how it had happened.
3. Empathise with the customer.
4. Give proof and compare how the present product or service can satisfy the customer.

Sometimes, the proof given for handling scepticism must be stronger than the one given when you are handling doubts. When customers who express scepticism are not handled correctly, you lose the sale.

Let us look at two scenarios related to customer scepticism.

Customer	This fabric seems very thin, and it may tear easily.
Salesperson	No, Sir, this is a micro-fibre cloth and strong, even used by football players.
Customer	Well, I do not play football, but I need something strong and durable. We need good material for uniforms.

Salesperson	You do not have to worry, Sir, let me show you. It is difficult to tear this fabric. It is exceptionally durable.
Customer	No, I am not happy... it is too thin. Show me something thicker, or I will go and buy from somewhere else.
Salesperson	You will not be able to get thicker material in micro-fibre. Maybe you should take cotton or polyester cotton.
Customer	Well, I like this material and do not want any other fabric. They will be heavier.

Now, let us see an alternate way of handling scepticism.

Customer	This fabric seems very thin, and it may tear easily.
Salesperson	This is a micro-fibre cloth and it is strong. May I understand why you feel it will tear easily?
Customer	Well, our delivery people carry a lot of packages with sharp objects, and we do not want them tearing and stitching their uniforms often.
Salesperson	I understand, Sir, let me show you...it is exceedingly difficult to tear this fabric. It is exceptionally durable. Even football players use it on the field and during workouts.
Customer	No, I am not happy, it is too thin. Show me something thicker, or I will go and buy from somewhere else.

Salesperson	Have you used this fabric before, Sir?
Customer	Yes, we have used a similar kind of fabric before, and it kept tearing all the time.
Salesperson	May I know what the fabric was and could I see a sample?
Customer	Yes, I have a sample piece here, as a matter of fact.
Salesperson	Sir, this fabric is thin, regular polyester. What we are suggesting is micro-fibre and tightly woven. Do check the fabric by trying to tear it. You will find the fabric suggested by us is tear-resistant.
Customer	Ok. You need to give us a guarantee.
Salesperson	I am sorry, Sir, we cannot guarantee regular wear and tear and accidental damages. I could certainly show you the quality standards of this fabric so you can check and compare. What do you say?
Customer	Ok, I will take this.

Well, sceptics will need a lot of proof and persuasion. A sure way of reducing their scepticism is to understand their experiences and show how things can be different with what you propose.

> *Try to understand the experience of sceptical customers. First empathise, and then show how the present experience is different from the previous one.*

11

How To Negotiate With the Customer

What is negotiation? It is a formal discussion between two people (here, the customer and the salesperson) with the purpose of reaching an agreement. Negotiations are done between buyers and sellers when they want to convert a 'no' to a 'yes'.

Most salespeople fear negotiations. "Is it good to negotiate?", "Will negotiation lead to a confrontation?", "Will not negotiating lead to standoffs?", and "Am I being rude when I am negotiating?" These are some of the doubts that arise in a salesperson's mind when they are confronted by their buyers, who always try to negotiate. The fear of negotiating must be exorcised from the salesperson's mind. Negotiations are intrinsic to the selling process. Negotiations are always a good way to improve mutual trust. Remember, Thomas Jefferson famously said, "In life, you do not get what you deserve, you get what you negotiate."

The first step for negotiating is saying NO when the customer makes an unrealistic request; one which you are certain you cannot meet easily. Most salespeople fear asserting themselves and accepting the customer's request. So, they end up giving commitments they cannot keep. To fulfil these commitments, they make several false promises and eventually lose the customer's trust. Remember, the customer's trust is never lost when you say NO. No order is lost overnight just because you have said NO. If an order is really lost by saying NO without the customer giving you a second chance, then, that customer does not want a relationship with you. It is better to say NO to that customer and lose the relationship rather than keep a false relationship going, as that will lead nowhere.

Remember, the fundamental task in selling is to build trust and nurture relationships. Saying NO is good when you cannot do something. But the crucial factor to keep in mind is that **how** you say NO.

While saying NO, never say NO abruptly, in one shot. Use multiple stages to say NO.

Let us see how this is done.

If a customer asks you to deliver a pizza in 10 minutes and you are sure that this is not possible, and you say, "No, Sir, it is impossible to deliver in 10 minutes," you are not putting in any effort to satisfy the customer's needs.

Consider the conversation below:

Customer	I need a 9-inch pizza, soft crust, plain topping.
Salesperson	Fine, Sir, we will send it in 30 minutes.
Customer	I need it in 10 minutes. Please send it fast.
Salesperson	No, Sir, it is impossible to deliver in 10 minutes.

Now let us see how NO can be said in stages.

Customer	I need a 9-inch pizza, soft crust.
Salesperson	Fine, Sir, we will send it in 30 minutes.

Customer	I need it in 10 minutes, please, send it fast.
Salesperson	Where is it to be delivered, Sir?
Customer	At the address you wrote down.
Salesperson	I am sorry, Sir, it will not be possible in 10 minutes. It will take us at least 10 minutes to bake the pizza and another 10 minutes to deliver.
Customer	I am in a hurry. I have a meeting to go to after lunch.
Salesperson	We could try to speed up and try to make the delivery in 15 minutes though we normally take 20 minutes. Hope that is ok.
Customer	Ok, but make it fast.

How to say NO correctly

What did the salesperson do here? Let us go through the simple steps he followed:
1. Apologised for saying NO.
2. Gave the reason behind it.
3. Offered what was possible. And informed the customer that this was something that was not usually done.

By doing this, you are inviting the customer to negotiate a mid-agreement. By saying, "No" or "It is not possible," you are not giving this chance at all. By saying NO gradually, the customer also feels that you are trying to meet their expectation though it is difficult for you. Then they start wondering if they are being unreasonable with you and have demanded something that is not possible at all.

So, the three stages of saying NO are:

Stage 1

1. Empathise—say sorry.
2. Say why it is not possible—give the reason.
3. Say what you could try—give an alternative.

If the customer does not agree with the alternative:

Stage 2

1. Again, apologise.
2. Say you will revert, but it is difficult (without raising expectations).
3. Come back with another alternative, a revised one, if possible.

If the customer still persists and maintains the old position:

Stage 3

1. Apologise and show in your behaviour that you are really sorry about what the customer is going through.
2. Offer the best possible solution and say politely that modifying it is not possible.
3. Try to convince the customer. If that is not possible, ask for a chance to do better next time.

What is empathy?

Empathy involves putting yourself in the customer's position. How can you show empathy? You need to first understand the emotional state of the customer and then show empathy when you say NO. By saying NO casually you create an opportunity for the customer to move away from you.

I am reminded of an anecdote that one of my close friends often shares to describe one's behaviour and state of mind while showing empathy.

An old beggar with one leg always begged at a particular traffic signal. One day, he found a motorist who was waiting for the signal to turn green. The beggar said he had a missing leg and was old and had nobody to care for him. The motorist just ignored the beggar and looked at the signal, waiting for it to turn green.

Soon a second motorist came to a stop at the beggar's signal. The beggar narrated the same story. The second motorist looked at him and started blaming the civic authorities for not taking the beggar away to a home for the aged.

A third motorist then arrived at the signal. He saw the beggar and listened to his story. He took a dollar out of his pocket and gave it to the beggar. He was expressionless and he gave the money as if it were the solution to the beggar's problems.

Along came a fourth motorist. This person listened to the beggar's tale. He asked some questions to understand the beggar's situation better. He wondered what would happen to him if he grew as old as the beggar, and was incapacitated. He gave the beggar a dollar too.

The first motorist did not show empathy, but **apathy**. In the previous example, if the pizza delivery person's reply to the customer asking for a five-minute pizza had been, "No, Sir, it will take 20 minutes," he would have been showing **apathy**.

The second motorist did not show empathy, but **antipathy,** which is to say, he meant to show he had nothing to do with the beggar, and the man was somebody else's problem. In the previous example, if the pizza delivery person had said, "I could deliver in five minutes, but the cook will take 15 minutes," he would have been showing antipathy.

The third motorist showed **sympathy,** not empathy. In the previous example, if the pizza delivery person had said, "Fine, Sir, we will try to send you the pizza in five minutes," he would be showing sympathy, but might be letting the customer down by overcommitting.

The fourth motorist displayed the **emotional traits for empathy**. He put himself in the beggar's place, thought about it, and then helped him. In the previous instance, if the pizza delivery person could have tried to understand the reasons for the customer's hurry, empathised and checked how he could help, and then given a reply he would have won the customer's heart.

Feeling the right emotion helps you to display the appropriate empathetic expression, which is important when you are dealing with people who are upset.

Showing the right empathetic feeling is also useful when a customer is extremely upset with your product or service. If dissent is not matched by emoting the right empathetic feeling, it grows into anger. Handling dissent well prevents the person from getting angry.

Whenever there is an angry customer your main weapon to manage the customer is the ability to show empathy. This diffuses the anger in them. It is no use arguing or proposing solutions when somebody is angry.

Consider the following scenario that unfolded in the open-air seating area of a coffee shop.

A customer was just about to drink his coffee when he noticed a fly in his drink.

The customer went ballistic and yelled at the steward, "What do you think is going on here? I only ordered coffee, not vitamins in the form of flies. I thought this chain was very good at maintaining hygiene, pest control, and so on."

The steward tried to defend himself by saying that there was no fly when he served the coffee. This response made the customer angrier. He swore that he would never come back to the coffee shop. And that he would also spread the word on social media.

The steward offered to fetch him a fresh cup of coffee. This was a big mistake as the customer thought the place was serving unhygienic food and drink. And the steward made it worse by offering him more of the same instead of empathising with him. He walked out of the coffee shop, swearing and shouting in front of all the other customers.

So, what happened here?

Was it the steward's mistake that a fly landed in the customer's coffee?

People get angry for many reasons. The steward could not afford to reason with the customer and negotiate the best solution as the customer was furious and not prepared to listen to any reasoning or accept a solution.

Angry customers cannot be negotiated with and will not be open to solutions. What can you do in such situations? You need to diffuse their anger first. When customers are angry, they are not thinking clearly before speaking. They are looking for an outlet to vent their anger and usually that target is the salesperson.

So, how does the salesperson deal with this? Can he just stay silent and stare at the angry person, hoping the anger will go away? That is precisely what the salesperson should not do. When an angry person sees a target on whom to vent his anger and the said target is merely staring at him with no expression, he gets angrier. The blank stare and the strategy of waiting for the anger to subside will be seen as apathy and make the angry person feel worse.

So, you cannot offer reasons and you cannot remain silent, waiting for the anger to disappear. What can you do instead?

Two emotions are used for this. Active listening by moving the body forward to indicate you really care. You need to display patience, empathy, and understanding here.

A person who is angry and is shouting will have a raised voice and a faster rate of speech. Also, the gaps between sentences will be short. The angry person just blurts out what is on their mind without thinking. One way to make out that a person's anger is subsiding is to observe whether the pitch is coming down, the gaps between sentences are becoming longer, and if the customer is pausing and speaking. Let the anger subside. After waiting for a four-second pause, you can respond with an apology.

If there is no angry retort to this apology, you should follow up with a positive statement such as, "This is something that never happens. I'm sure we can work out something to avoid this," and then request the person to calm down.

A solution can be suggested after a gap. The gap allows the angry person to think and sometimes, after some thought the person becomes apologetic about their outburst. Once the anger is vented, the person is in a better state of mind to listen to a suggestion.

In the coffee shop scenario where the customer got angry about the fly, instead of arguing or offering suggestions, if the steward had said sorry and brought a second cup saying, "I made a fresh one, Sir. Also checked on the pest control system. We need to make sure to spray a disinfectant in the outdoor seating area too. I'm really sorry about that."

This would make the customer feel less angry and he would change his mind about not visiting the cafe again.

He would also feel sorry about having put the steward in an embarrassing position by shouting at him and being abusive in public.

The technique to be used to handle an angry customer is called—LEAPS.

L—*Listen* with the right body language and match the emotion.

E—Show *empathy*. Listen and empathise.

A—*Apologise* softly once you sense the person's anger has been vented.

P—Make a *positive statement*. Do not argue or become angry.

S—*Suggest* what can be done only after a while. Do not offer a solution straightaway, as an angry customer will not listen to the voice of reason when they are fuming. Wait for them to calm down.

We often see chaotic scenes at airports while waiting for a flight and hear people shouting at the boarding gate agent when a flight is delayed. Most of the time, the agent do their best to diffuse the situation. But when the agent asks, "What can I do if the weather is not fine?", arguments ensue. These lead to even more frustration and more arguments.

Other passengers also get involved and start getting annoyed by the agent's responses and soon it blows up into a full-fledged fight between passengers and the agent. It does not augur well at all when the agent does not help them to vent their anger. If they did that, the crowd would back off. And those passengers empathising with the agent's plight would try to pacify the ones who were angry and the situation would improve.

Now you know the importance of saying NO in stages. Now, let us see how that is possible.

First stage

1. Understand the reason behind the anger, say sorry, and show empathy.
2. Give the reason why what is requested by the person is not possible.
3. Say what is possible and check if it is ok.

If the customer does not agree to the alternative proposed by you, then you need to move to the second stage of saying NO.

Second stage

1. Apologise—"I am sorry, Sir."
2. Take some time—"Give me 10 minutes let me see what best I can do."

Third stage

1. Offer the best possible option.
2. Wait for the customer to agree.
3. If the customer becomes unreasonable and does not budge this is the best that can be done and close.

> *Before you say NO, understand the customer's request better, empathise, and then say NO, and give the reason why their request cannot be met and suggest what is possible.*

It is better to try and do your best and say NO in stages, showing the customer that you are putting in some effort. Do not make a commitment you cannot keep. You cannot say NO in stages unless you make a habit of 'underpromising and overdelivering'. Let us consider a conversation between a car salesperson and a customer.

Customer	So, when am I getting the car delivered?
Salesperson	In four days, Sir, as we had promised you.
Customer	But I need it tomorrow as I am going on a vacation. I need it urgently.
Salesperson	I am sorry, Sir, the car has been sent to our workshop for a polish. It will take two days for the paint to dry, and then we need to check the car. I am afraid four days is the best we can do.
Customer	No, no, please try and understand my situation. All reservations for hotels and my travel are made. I cannot afford a rental.
Salesperson	I am sorry, Sir. As per our policy and what we just told you, four days will be needed.
Customer	Then, I will cancel the order.
Salesperson	That is your prerogative, Sir. We don't want to give you a promise we can't keep.
Customer	Ok, I will try another reseller. Thanks.

In this scenario, both the salesperson and the customer were sticking to their positions and finding reasons to do so. Most customers like to be inflexible. They feel that if they put pressure on salespeople to relent, salespeople will succumb. They become habitual bargainers. Note that I am using the word 'bargaining', not 'negotiating'. Bargaining is done on one variable with fixed starting positions. Negotiations are done by showing flexibility and an intent by both parties to move forward. This is possible only if the NO is said well and in stages.

12

How To Negotiate Successfully

Before you learn about the skills needed for sales negotiations, you need to be clear about the difference between negotiating and bargaining. As you learnt in the previous chapter, bargaining is done on one variable, maybe the price. It can be quite a simple variable.

An example of bargaining is given below.

Customer	How much do these apples cost?
Salesperson	Two euros a pound, Sir.
Customer	Two euros? Wow! That is way too much.
Salesperson	How much would you pay for these?
Customer	Well, I think I bought these in a supermarket for a euro or so.
Salesperson	Ma'am, 1.7 euros is the best I can offer these at.
Customer	That is way too much. I will give you 1.3 euros. Thirty cents more than the ones in the supermarket.
Salesperson	Ok. Best price. I am sure you will like them.
Customer	I will try these out.

What happened in this case? Both the salesperson and the customer were bargaining around the price. There was only one variable involved in the discussion, 'price'. Frequently, when there is bargaining around just one variable, the decision to agree or not to agree happens fast. Also, if there is an agreement, it concludes midway between the positions taken by the two people negotiating.

Sometimes, when we start to bargain, we forget to evaluate who has won and who has not. But is that important? And why it is important to evaluate a WIN–WIN?

Mainly, this is because sales negotiations should end in a trustworthy relationship. It does not matter who has won. It matters if both parties have been able to strike a long-term relationship even if there is a WIN–LOSE or a LOSE–WIN temporary agreement. Then, they will have opportunities to move to a WIN–WIN over a period of time. Else, the bargaining will conclude with both the salesperson and the customer feeling that they were better off not bargaining and this will lead to a LOSE–LOSE situation.

So, what is the difference between negotiating and bargaining? Negotiation happens when two or more people try to reach an agreement by moving towards each other from their fixed positions to reach an agreement. Negotiation is a process of converting a 'no' to a 'yes'. You cannot start a negotiation unless you say NO first. There is no negotiation required when there is an agreement.

Negotiating, unlike bargaining, is done when there is more than one variable. While bargaining, closure is done fast, moving to conclusion without either party sensing and feeling if there has been a WIN–WIN or if trust was built. It involves several interactions and even sparring, so that both feel satisfied with the results and agreements.

Let us go back to the example we had taken up for bargaining. Pay attention to how the customer and the salesperson directed the bargaining to a negotiation.

Customer	How much do these apples cost?
Salesperson	Two euros a pound, Sir.
Customer	Two euros? Wow! That is way too much.
Salesperson	How much would you pay for these?
Customer	Well…I think I bought these in a supermarket for a euro or so.
Salesperson	Sir, I agree, you do get apples from different places with different tastes and quality standards. These apples are fresh, and I personally get them from Poland. They are grown in my cousin's farm. Please sample one.
Customer	Yes, it tastes good. But I don't think they should cost that much. Poland is not far away, so 1.3 euros is reasonable.
Salesperson	1.3 euros do not cover my cost, Sir.
Customer	I will take 2 pounds, but I will pay only 1.5 euros.
Salesperson	Ok, I will sell you 2 pounds for 1.5 euros. Only for you. As a special case. Please don't tell anybody, else I will have to shut shop.
Customer	I promise not to tell a soul. I will come back for more if they are good.

Well, first of all, the discussion involved more than one variable than the price. The salesperson started the dialogue with quality and country of origin as variables and led the customer to quantity. The customer felt good about buying a quality product and was happy he had got some price benefit. The salesperson felt ok, as he was able to sell more and hope that he had acquired a customer who would come back as he had built a relationship with the man.

So, to start a negotiation, two people should have more than one variable to negotiate about and they must understand each other's positions on all the variables. Negotiating involves deeper understanding and more discussions than bargaining.

Many people are confused about whether or not it is good to negotiate. Negotiations are often considered rude and impolite. Many customers dislike negotiating and accepting the conditions offered by the other person. But, by not negotiating, you may lose the chance to build a closer relationship. Without negotiating, the trust established will be low. It is always better to negotiate and close the different positions after understanding each other, than to avoid negotiating and have a poor understanding of each other.

I am reminded of a pertinent quote about negotiation which I often share with my team: "In business as in life, you do not get what you deserve. You get what you negotiate." Many things are assumed unless you negotiate. Only then do you get what you really want. If you take this road, the other person also understands what you want better.

The great John F. Kennedy rightly said, "Let us never negotiate out of fear. But let us never fear to negotiate."

> *Negotiation is the art of transforming a 'no' to a 'yes'.*
> *It is the art of arriving at agreements.*

Types of negotiation

Most people avoid to negotiate because they are scared of the consequences. They think that when you start negotiating for something, the other person will end up thinking that you are a cheapster. Ask any salesperson and they will tell you that it is standard practice for a customer to negotiate with them. Sometimes, salespersons will start to defend their price and position and begin to argue. This may lead the buyer to think that the salesperson is becoming unreasonable, indifferent to their needs, or simply does not need them. Buyers will often read this as a conflict that has to be sorted out. Soon, they will start using tactics to negotiate and put the salesperson in a very defensive and tough position.

When this happens, the salesperson either starts arguing and becomes defensive, or submissive. These responses are not good for building mutual trust and long-term relationships. This type of negotiation is popularly known as the red-type.

Often, when salespeople are led into negotiations by buyers on the price, they fear losing the order or the business so much that they relent or become very submissive. On sensing this, buyers see an opportunity to push salespeople to relent even more till they feel defeated and start to pamper the buyers. This does not strengthen trust or the relationship. Salespeople will start to hate confronting the buyers and prefer to avoid any discussion. Buyers keep pushing till both parties lose. Negotiations of this type are not beneficial to either side. This kind of negotiation is popularly known as the blue-type.

The ideal type of negotiation is when both salespeople and customers are persuasive and assertive. They try to win each other's trust. They spar, parry, and trade positions. They try to give and take and ensure that trust and the relationship are not affected. They constantly look at long-term WIN–WIN.

It is often said that negotiations are conducted like the two hands of a scissors. They are sharp and flexible, and they move smoothly. They do not hurt each other but work together to get the job done.

To summarise:

Red-type

Here hard balling is done, and tough positions are reached. Tactics used are manipulative, calculative, and aggressive.

Blue-type

Cooperative-type, where both are eager to please, pamper, and reach agreements by pleading, retreating, relenting, and ultimately not building trust.

Purple-type

Persuasive-type, where both are persuading each other conditionally, trading, giving, and taking in an assertive and a respectful and constructive way.

So, if it is a good idea to negotiate and build transparent relationships, the next question is 'when should you negotiate?' Is it always good to negotiate when there is a different position taken? Is it essential to negotiate if you are the buyer? Most buyers think it is part of their job to negotiate and get the best deal for themselves. I would argue that negotiation is worth it only if some benefit comes of it. As mentioned earlier, bargaining happens fast, but the process of negotiation is quite slow. It demands time and effort. So, it is best not to jump in and negotiate when the gains are not big enough. Monetary gains are a major consideration. You can also negotiate to build a better relationship.

One way of deciding whether it is worth negotiating is to visualise the gains. There are other ways of building relationships than negotiating. Many people become impulsive negotiators while trying to get a bargain. They think that the other person is always trying to cheat them and rob them of the best deal. So, they feel the need to negotiate no matter what. We Indians have this bargain fixation so deeply embedded in our system that many of us buy things only when we see a discount being offered. Indians are also compulsive bargainers. We love it—rich and poor!

When I visit Africa and Egypt, I observe the skills the hawkers there use to sell their products. Many of them need to sell, but they sell badly. The post-Corona era will bring out the best in salespeople everywhere. It is quite likely that supply will exceed demand many times. But salespeople should never show desperation to sell and negotiate (or bargain). They need to sense and feel whether it is worth it. Visualise the gains. Assess the brand value gain or erosion while negotiating. Anyway, salespeople need to negotiate only when the customer says NO—when they are grappling with fixed positions.

Salespeople normally hate negotiating. Usually, when they sense a buyer is trying to bargain around the price, they have two reactions—either they freeze and grow silent or they say they have to check with their bosses, superiors—the people who they report to. Or worse, they stay silent, which can be taken for a yes.

This is the worst mistake they can make. When the salesperson freezes, the buyer senses that they can win. It is similar to what happens when a cobra rears its head and hisses at its prey. The prey freezes, making itself an easy target for the cobra.

If the salesperson says they must revert, the buyer assumes it is possible to get a better price, and the salesperson only has to check and get an approval. So, the buyer gets all fired up to put pressure on the salesperson. So, both these positions used by salespersons are no good.

As a rule, when the buyer starts a negotiation, the seller should never start negotiating. The seller must assert. Say NO to the position taken by the buyer. Give reasons and suggest an alternative. Be flexible with the alternative and say you must check what is possible. You have learnt how to assert in an earlier chapter.

> *As a general rule, never start to negotiate when the other person tries to do so.*
> *When somebody tries to negotiate with you, it means they are better prepared than you.*

It is always good to back off when the other person is well-prepared. So, when is the perfect time to start? There is no perfect time. All it takes is some preparation. Depending on the importance of the variable being negotiated, it can be started as soon as—

You have the **power of state-of-mind.** This means that you have no fear of failure. You are clear that the negotiation will be helpful in strengthening the relationship or there will be benefits in moving forward in the sale even if there are no monetary gains. The mind should be clear about WHY the negotiation is being done, including the purpose, the benefits, and the results.

You have the **power of agreement.** Enough thought has to be given to whether it is worthwhile to negotiate when there is no chance of an agreement. Is it worth negotiating around a lost cause? Power of agreement relates to having something in hand which can help you gain something from the other person. It means that you have a chance of winning.

You have the **power of monopoly.** When you know you have something in terms of features and service advantages which your competitor does not possess, it gives you better leverage to assert and get something from the customer. We have discussed competitive differentiators and power earlier.

You have the **power of taking a risk.** When you negotiate, there is always a risk. You also need to contend with the fact that things may not work out the way you want. You may lose more than you gain. Sometimes, you may lose more than you gain monetarily, but may have done that deliberately in order to build a relationship. There are many intangible factors that may be important. The person who negotiates must have the necessary 'psychic safety' with them when they negotiate. This refers to the freedom the negotiator must gracefully give and sometimes lose without being penalised for it later. Some people fear to take risks and are afraid of failure. They may not negotiate successfully. (Read *Above and Beyond—How to Build Impactful Businesses*, to better understand the concept of psychic safety, which ensures that everybody wins (www.abovebeyond.in).

You have the **power of expertise.** This goes without saying. You cannot negotiate without having knowledge of or expertise in what you are negotiating. When selling a product or service, you must know everything about what you are offering. You must be confident of what you say when you negotiate. Confidence matters. Your body language, voice, and confidence while communicating are crucial factors.

You have the **power to take decisions.** Frequently, a boss will respond to a salesperson who comes back to them with the news that the customer wants to negotiate the prices for an offer by saying, "Go ahead and negotiate." However, the salesperson will not be given any power to take decisions. What this does is handicap the salesperson's scope to negotiate. Every time a customer makes a request on the price or any other variable, the salesperson checks with the boss. The customer senses this and knows that the negotiating salesperson is weak. They go for the jugular, and this leads to a WIN–LOSE in favour of the customer. It is no good going into a negotiation where the limits are not fixed by the authority, and the negotiating salesperson does not have the power to take decisions on the spot. This is the 'psychic safety' we referred to earlier.

You have the **power of persuasion.** This is my favourite buzzword these days. It is a vast and complex subject. While negotiating is an art, there are enough tactics and processes you can adopt to sharpen your skills. Persuasion skills are different. Persuading someone to see your point of view depends on reading the situation in front of you and presenting your proposition in such a way that the other person is convinced. The chapter on building rapport explains how rapport-building leads to winning trust and often succeeds in persuading customers. We have used personality-mapping skills in building rapport to persuade and close with different personalities. These skills are called the power to persuade.

Let me share an experience I had in Bali, Indonesia. I travelled to Indonesia to hold a training session and when I had a three-day weekend, I visited Bali. I was staying on my own in Kuta, a crowded touristy locality where I frequently walked around to find good restaurants. One night, when I stepped out of the hotel where I was staying, a man in a flowery shirt sporting a broad smile accosted me.

"Sir, you want some girls? We have some nice girls," he said.

Having travelled widely in Southeast Asia, I was not shocked. Smiling, I replied, "No, I don't want any girls."

The guy looked hurt, but he came back in a while and started walking behind me. He waited for me to turn around and make eye contact, and said, "Sir, I understand. Do you want boys?" He gave me a frozen smile and added, "We have really nice boys".

Again, I was not shocked. However, I was not swayed by his perseverance. "No," I said. "I don't like boys."

The man would not give up. "What do you like, Sir? I can get you anything you want."

I dismissed him by saying, "I want a horse."

He was stumped. He slunk away, but not for long. He came up to me again, meeting me with a smile, at a crossing where I had to stop. He was apologetic this time. He said, "Sorry, Sir, I couldn't get a horse, but we have a girl who looks like a horse."

We burst out laughing.

Persuasion is the art of prevailing on people to agree with you not by forcing them to accept your point of view, but by urging them to and listing reasons with benefits to do so.

Renowned public speaker Rob Biesenbach once said, "A buyer will listen to a variety of sales pitches and weigh the pros and cons of each seller, but will ultimately be moved by feelings of trust. So, emotion doesn't just drive decision-making, it unlocks it. If you want to make a person to agree with you, you need to make them feel something."

You have the **power of attitude.** Attitude is everything when you set out to negotiate with a person. You may have the knowledge and necessary skills, which you have honed over time, but when your attitude is not right, refrain from negotiating. Your attitude is controlled primarily by how you feel about the person with whom you are negotiating. It is easy to say that you should love your opponent, and respect your rival in sporting activities, but difficult to practise it in real life.

Attitude encompasses a set of emotions, beliefs, and behaviours towards the person with whom you are negotiating. If you and the person with whom you are negotiating with have different personalities, it makes it all the more important to recognise this and deal with the person accordingly.

To sum up, what you need before you start negotiating are the following: you must have power, the time to negotiate, and the information. Remember, it takes time to negotiate since it cannot be done quickly like bargaining. Many variables must be considered and processed, data collected on different variables, and perceptions understood before beginning to negotiate.

This is called the **PTI** of negotiation—Power Time Information.

> Before starting a negotiation make sure you have POWER, and you are well-prepared, and have the TIME and INFORMATION on hand.

Power is not a collateral—something you have because you do not trust the other person or something that is obtained as you do not trust the other person, who may be a stranger. Let us understand collaterals with the help of this humourous anecdote about banks.

Bank Clerk	What are you going to do with the money?
Customer	I am going to go to the city and sell my handmade jewellery.
Bank Clerk	Do you have collateral?
Customer	What's collateral?
Bank Clerk	Collateral is something of value that can cover the amount of the loan. For example, do you have a car?
Customer	I have a 20-year-old tractor.
Bank Clerk	That will not do. Do you have livestock?
Customer	Yes, I have a few cows.
Bank Clerk	How old are they?
Customer	Three years old and yielding milk.

After some negotiations, the customer and the bank clerk settle on the cows as collateral. The clerk does all the paperwork and gives the customer $5,000.

A few weeks later, the customer returns to the bank, walks up to the same clerk, takes out a huge wad of bills, and returns the loan.

Bank Clerk	I see your jewellery sold well. What are you going to do with the rest of the money?
Customer	I will keep it under my pillow.
Bank Clerk	No need to do that. You can make a deposit in our bank.

Customer	What is a deposit?
Bank Clerk	A deposit is when you give money to the bank, the bank cares for it, and when it is time, you can come back to the bank and take your money.
Customer	(After thinking for a moment) And what does the bank have as collateral?

The customer is peeved as the bank wants collateral in order to lend him money, but does not think it is important to give collateral when the bank wants the customer's deposit. Basically, it stems from the fact that banks do not trust customers, but want customers to trust banks.

Power, on the other hand, is not a collateral. It is something you have that the customer wants badly. This can be derived from the value provided to the customer. Value, we have seen earlier, is provided by salespersons to their customers if needs are better understood and satisfied. For commodity products, there is no power in negotiation. The product is bought on the price. There is no power. The business can go any day. Products sold only on the price and no other value or power (something the customer wants badly), will be bought from others in the future who can offer better prices.

Power can also be built through a relationship. The customer wants to build a relationship with you for something other than the product you are negotiating about. Some other service, something you have done in the past, or something in the relationship that has been invested well. For example, an old customer has walked into your store to buy a bag and could not find what he wanted, and so he leaves. After he walked away, you enquired about the availability of the product he wanted and called him to inform him and make sure he got it.

By doing this you have invested in this relationship. You may have acquired a power with this customer to influence him in the future.

There is one other thing that negotiation experts feel you should plan to have, and that is BATNA. This applies to all kinds of negotiations.

BATNA (**B**est **A**lternative **T**o **N**o **A**greement): Simply put, it is something you will use in a negotiation when things are breaking down or turning sour; in other words, you and the customer are moving away from a decision or your back is against the wall.

BATNA is a power you have on hand. But it should not be used often. Else, the customer will develop a counter for it.

Consider this example. A salesperson is selling a car to a customer. They realise that the customer has taken a great liking for the car's comfortable seats and the ventilation (cooling and heating) they provide. The customer has a back problem and needs this. No competitor offers this feature.

This feature can become a BATNA or a power in a negotiation. But use the BATNA-value sparingly. Use it only when the negotiation is breaking down, when there is no agreement, or when the customer is walking away without agreeing to what has been offered so far.

Over-use of a BATNA in sales situations negates its power. The value is lost. Having a BATNA or power is like holding higher value cards like the ace of spades or king of spades and using them when you must win or generate a WIN–WIN.

A BATNA is normally not required when a negotiation starts. It can be arrived at while negotiating.

It is also not always necessary to have a BATNA. A golden silence accompanied by keen perception of the other person's emotions and matching them could work better during a negotiation. It is also advisable to take a break and have some time to think calmly.

> *Before starting any negotiation make sure you have POWER—something the other person wants badly and a BATNA—Best Alternative To No Agreement.*

Information is collected before you start a negotiation and during it. We will discuss the need for information later. Information can be grouped as follows:

1. Understand and populate 'negotiation variables'.
2. Establish overall limits for all the variables.
3. Establish needs, wants, and desires.
4. Prioritise the hierarchy around what to negotiate.
5. Research all the data on competition, history of customer interactions, and their past experiences.
6. Collate in the negotiation grid before starting.

Let us take the example of Stephen to understand how this is done.

Stephen is a salesperson who sells jewellery door-to-door and he specialises in custom-made jewellery for special occasions and weddings. He networks with many jewellery designers and manufacturers to source them. His value proposition is that his designs are one-of-a-kind.

He received an enquiry on his website from a customer who liked one of his designs and wanted to customise it. He called up the customer and drove down 100 miles to possibly seal the deal. The offer from him was $5,000 for a set with earrings and a choker of matching design. He sensed in the call that the customer was not too happy about the price. He did some background research on the customer and found out from her Facebook account that Miriam Rashida was a socialite from Egypt originally and married to an American. She had a country home which was far away from the city, but she frequently travelled around the world.

She had wanted to negotiate on the phone and close, but Stephen wanted to take his time. He needed time to prepare and research and check with designers in Europe and manufacturers in Thailand.

As he was driving, he was thinking about how important this business was. It was the post-Corona era. Business had been bad for the last six months. Nobody partied. People practised social distancing. They craved company. Lifestyles were drastically different as people had gone back to the basics. Lives were simplified out of necessity. Still, he hoped Rashida had returned to the old ways. He needed people to buy designer jewellery with great designs instead of the run-of-the-mill stuff from shopping malls and stores.

Stephen mentally prepared himself for the day's negotiation. He realised the overwhelming need to take Rashida's mind off from just the price. It was the mentality these days. Everybody looked for a bargain even for products they liked and wanted badly. Impulse buying was fast disappearing. People had decided to be careful. Corona had put a scare into everybody and they were keen to stash away their money safely. In many countries, gold was the safest investment as it had appreciated annually by 12% on an average for the last 40 years. No wonder it was considered safe.

The design Stephen had in mind had less of gold. It was 14-karat gold, that is, the percentage of gold in the alloy was lesser than that of most jewellery. But the design was intricate. He needed to explain the design features, the workmanship, the exclusivity, how Rashida would be able to stand out and be noticed, and how there is no other design like this available in the market. Her friends would envy her. The diamonds were rare, uniquely cut, almost flawless, and truly worthy of a queen. These thoughts consumed Stephen as he drove on.

Rashida was old school. She would understand the importance of flaunting the matching set in her next party for her grand fundraiser. Her daughter would not. She would best like to get herself a new iPhone.

Let us see how Stephen could negotiate this. He needs to list out the negotiating variables as the first step:

1. Gold purity and value. Likely benefits in investing in gold.
2. Design intricacy and workmanship.
3. Accessorising—complements party wear.
4. His warranty against manufacturing defects.
5. Exchange benefits—returns from gold appreciations—new value of gold versus old value when it was bought.
6. Exclusivity.
7. Flaunt value.
8. An opportunity to try out a sample before ordering.
9. Time taken to deliver it.
10. Landed price that includes taxes and delivery charges.

(Always put the price at the end. Though this is an important aspect of clinching the deal, it stops you from bargaining and short-circuiting the whole relationship.)

These variables evolve during the sales negotiation process. Some will be added, and some will be discarded. Starting with a strong set of negotiating variables helps in organising your thoughts while planning a negotiation.

Sometimes it is also good to prioritise these in the order of importance. This helps in collecting data and perceptions around the variables. For example, the salesperson may think that buying an accessory to enhance a person's looks for a party may be important, but it may not be important for the customer. She may be thinking exclusivity is more important. So, during the negotiation, it will emerge which factor is more important for the customer and which one for the salesperson.

> *Thinking and preparing about a set of negotiation variables is an important thing to do even before starting to negotiate.*

Rashida	Thanks for coming over to show me the jewellery set I liked. I hope we can settle the price a little lower as I feel 5,000 dollars is a bit too much.
Stephen	Sure, Ma'am, I agree. Price is important. First, I would like to show you the set. May I request you to first try it?
Rashida	No, no…don't bother. I don't want to try it. I have seen the design and used similar products. I just need something new to wear for the family function next week. Most of my relatives have seen my old jewellery. I cannot wear what I have worn before. I want something new.
Stephen	I agree you need to wear something new. It should also be exclusive. Let me explain what I have selected for you. It is designed especially for party wear.
Rashida	Yes, but it is expensive and I can't spend so much. I can afford to spend only 3,500 dollars, so please don't show it to me if you can't give it to me at 3,500 dollars.

Stephen	I understand, I can present two other sets. One for 2,500 dollars and the other for 3,500 dollars. I'm sure we can meet your price requirements and also find something which suits you. Allow me to present this piece, it was picked by you.
Rashida (wears the set)	It fits ok, looks ok too. But I don't think I need something so flashy, so I'll settle for this other one. My daughter also liked this design.
Stephen	Let me show you the features. See, this hand-enameling work is very exclusive and the artist is from France. See also the mesh work. That is a weaving technique with gold wires which is different and unique.
Rashida	Yes, I like this. But is it fragile and delicate? Will the gold wires get cut? Or snag if they get caught in something sharp?
Stephen	Absolutely not...but you need to be careful. Moreover, since it is handmade, it can be repaired. It is a partywear piece. Something your relatives will surely notice. Here is a brochure about the artist and his style and range.
Rashida	I'll keep this...if you don't mind. I will definitely read about the artist.
Stephen	How is the fitting? Another special feature of ours is that we custom-fit all our jewellery. We check the pressure points and make the modifications. After you put in an order, we will supply you with a similar piece master in copper and make the changes you suggest. Please feel free to suggest changes.

Rashida	Ok. I need it to be made a bit lighter.
Stephen	Fine, I have noted your request and will change the design to make it lighter.
Rashida	Otherwise it looks good. Except for the price. What can you do about that?
Stephen	The price is reasonable as it is handmade. Handmade designs can be rectified and modified. I will still give you 300 dollars off from 5,000 dollars. What do you say?
Rashida	Just 300 dollars off? Give me 1,000 dollars off at least and let us settle for 4,000 dollars.
Stephen	Ma'am, I don't have that much margin. Let me come back tomorrow and see what is the best possible option. What you are asking for looks very difficult though.

We can see that Stephen laid out all the variables on the table. He talked about design exclusivity, party wear, custom handmade pieces, changes to suit the customer, and the style factor with the French designer and his design. The flaunt value is what he thought would be the clincher.

He was not inflexible with the prices even when he sensed he could have closed the sale. He gave a marginal reduction in price to show his flexibility. He also showed that a reduction in price was difficult by saying he had no margins. He wanted the customer's expectation to be low on that front. He did not want the relationship to be taken to a WIN–LOSE even when he could close the sale with that. He preferred to let the customer feel he was trying to put in an effort to satisfy her price need.

Taking time is a good way of closing when there is an acceleration to close the deal with prices. It gives the impression that you are sensitive.

So, let us look at the stages of negotiation. Stephen was visiting the customer for the first time. His objective in this visit was to have a better understanding of the negotiating variables. This would help him plan the next stage of negotiation. This first step of negotiations, where both negotiators parry to find each other's expectations, is called 'broad-based negotiation'.

Broad-based negotiation is a nibbling-type, first-time negotiation. Here, all negotiating variables are discussed, but not in depth. This is done to gain understanding around negotiating variables and list what is important for whom. It is also done to find the limits of both sides around the variables.

Deep-penetration negotiation is normally started when a good idea is conceived around all the negotiating variables and limits, and what is important is adequately understood.

While conducting broad-based negotiation, it is important to sense and feel the customer's perceptions around the negotiating variables. It is also important to consider new variables the customer may introduce. Again, understand the new variables and check how important they are for the customer. For example, Rashida raised the importance of whether the jewellery would be fragile. Stephen needed to understand whether his customer had had an experience of her jewellery breaking off. Maybe this variable could prove to be important when he compared his designs with fragile general jewellery made in China and available at low prices in the markets. Maybe a BATNA could emerge from this.

After understanding negotiating variables, Stephen needed to plot them in a grid to plan his next moves.

Remember, broad-based negotiation is a preliminary negotiation. Here, all negotiating variables are discussed, but not in depth.

Deep penetration is done for subsequent negotiations. Here, the important negotiating variables are discussed deeply till a consensus is reached.

Let us see what a negotiation grid looks like.

Variable	Stephen's Limit/ Position	ZOPA (Zone of Possible Agreements)	Rashida's Limit/ Position
Gold investment value.	Has offered lower karatage (14k), which may not offer higher gold investing possibility.	Karatage may not be important.	Did not indicate she is buying to invest.
Design intricacy and workmanship.	Handmade and intricate.	If proof is given, she will be convinced.	Worried it could be fragile.
Accessorising —benefits with party wear.	Features like enamelling/ mesh work.	Existing design modified marginally to be lighter.	Seemed to deflect saying it was flashy, but liked the looks, wanted something lightweight.

His warranty against manufacturing defects.	Can be hand rectified, as it is handmade, not offered warranty.	May offer some warranty and agree to rectify if damaged in the future.	Concerned about damages.
Exclusivity with its looks.	Designer is French, exclusive.	Need to strengthen designer flaunt value.	Had shown interest. Kept catalogue.
Style elements and flaunt value.	One-of-its-kind-design, not supermarket stuff, even Cartier does not have.	Need to strengthen this variable offer this as unique advantage.	Seemed to accept this as important.
Trying out a prototype before she ordered and got it made.	Offer to make prototype to ensure correct fit and feel.	Can reach agreement.	Seemed to like it.
Time taken to deliver it. When did she need it to be delivered?	Needed to assess when and how badly she wants it.	Needed to assess when and how badly she wants it to be delivered at her house.	Needs for an event. Did not specify date.
Price expected.	$5,000.	$4,000–$4,700.	$3,500.

Once the negotiation grid is clear, it is easy to plan the negotiation. Normally, facts, arguments, and concessions are made around the variables. Both parties tend to move forward towards the zone of possible agreements (ZOPA).

After the limits and positions around the negotiating variables are made clear, it is time for deep-penetration negotiation. This is done to reach an agreement. If there is no consensus around a variable, it is wise to move towards another to negotiate. You can also relent from your position. This is called casting a discard. A 'discard' is something you can give away. It shows flexibility. While discarding something from your position, you can ask to take something. It is always good to give and take while negotiating.

Rashida	Hi, Stephen! Have you worked out the best prices for me? Look. I find your price of 5,000 dollars really high. I can't pay more than 3,000 dollars, but I am ready to buy if your price is around 4,000 dollars.
Stephen	Ma'am, I did some rework on whether it is possible to sell it to you at 4,000 dollars, but I don't want to remove any design elements, as you liked them. I hope we can settle on 4,500 dollars. It has been tough to reduce prices from 5,000 to 4,500 dollars. It is a unique design, handmade. And getting skilled jewellery craftsmen is so difficult.
Rashida	4,500 dollars is way above my budget of 3,000 dollars, and I have raised my offer from 3,000 dollars to 4,000 dollars. I'll buy that nice piece in Tiffany's I saw yesterday. It is good. They are a strong, aspiring, and a reliable brand.

Stephen	I do agree Tiffany's is good. But I thought you would have liked our exclusive designer piece that nobody else would own. I can offer you our other designs at 3,000 dollars which would be more common ones, but I wanted you to have the exclusive design you can flaunt.
Rashida	True, I like the design you are offering, but it is not affordable.
Stephen	Ma'am, I am trying to do the best with the prices. I will support you with modifications and any repairs, if it comes to that, free of cost. It is a delicate and also an exclusive piece. Your friends will especially notice it; you will be making a trendsetting style statement.
Rashida wears the set	Just this once, sell it to me at 4,000 dollars, and I don't want to haggle. It is not my nature. I will buy more from you next time and recommend you to all my friends.
Stephen	Please do, Ma'am. Let us settle it at 4,000 dollars then. I will make a prototype in a few days. You can try the prototype and check the comfort. I will make sure after you test it that the final piece is delivered two days before the party.
Rashida	Ok. And make sure they are light—the earrings, I mean.

Stephen	Absolutely. I have redesigned it like this (shows picture) without changing the gold content. I could have made it cheaper by altering it. But I wanted to ensure the design and the look are not compromised.
Rashida	Looks nice now.
Stephen	Please let us settle it at 4,000 dollars. With 50% advance now, and the balance after I deliver.
Rashida	Ok.

Notice carefully that Rashida was trying to close fast by bargaining around the price. Stephen sensed that she wanted the design badly, and exclusivity was important. However, she tried to create a smokescreen around what she wanted. She also tried to dangle a carrot by saying she would buy more and ask her friends to buy. She also told Stephen that if he did not relent on the price, she would buy from Tiffany's, and that was that!

These are the tactics used in sales negotiations. When tactics are used by buyers, salespeople normally do not have answers. They tend to relent and start losing out in that relationship. It is important to remember that there is no harm in countering those tactics.

It is a good sign if buyers start using tactics. This means that they are interested. Salespeople should recognise these tactics, and they should not feel they are losing.

When buyers start using tactics, it means that they want to negotiate a closure. And they want to buy badly.

Let us discuss in detail the countertactics that were used in the negotiation.

Rashida (starts bluffing)	4,500 dollars is way above my budget of 3,000 dollars, and I have come up to 4,000 dollars. This is quite not enough. I think I will end up buying that nice piece I saw at Tiffany's.
Stephen (sticks to his position)	I do agree. Tiffany's is good. I really thought you would have liked the exclusive designer piece which nobody else would have. I do have other designs at 3,000 dollars. But I wanted you to have the best.
Rashida	Just this time, and I don't want to haggle. It is not my style. I will buy more from you next time and recommend you to all my friends.
Stephen (thanks, but moves to close)	Please do, Ma'am. But do settle it. I will make a prototype in a few days, check the comfort, and make sure it is delivered to you two days before the party.

Most buyers use a recognisable set of tactics. Salespeople need to remember that these tactics are used to gain something and take the negotiations to bargaining. Normally, this revolves around the price or whatever feature the customer wants badly. If the customer wants something badly, then salespeople need not worry. They need to give a first impression that they are not intimidated. Then, they need to visualise what the customer wants. They should plan a BATNA but use it only if the negotiations are likely to fail. They can very effectively use a countertactic first and throw in other variables. If not, seek an adjournment to find more variables or power in the relationship. Remember, a good negotiator always yearns for a WIN–WIN in a relationship.

Some countertactics that you can use to deal with common customer tactics are given below.

Tactics	Countertactics
Making threats.	Tell customer you cannot decide. Seek clarifications.
Intimidation.	Stay calm. Restate position firmly.
Bluffing.	Call out their bluff. Refuse to agree—wait for reaction. Request evidence.
Offering something more later—higher volumes, more business.	Thank them for doing that. And then ask to close this.
Making emotional appeals.	Affirm commitment for a fair settlement.
Testing boundaries.	Be clear on boundaries. Clarify positions clearly.

Author Michael Michalko and international creative thinking expert relates an excellent story on negotiation:

A Franciscan monk who was a speaker at an international seminar about world peace was asked if successful negotiations between Israel and Palestine were ever possible. He called two young people to the microphone—a Palestinian boy and a Jewish Israeli boy.

"Imagine you were brothers," he told them. "Your father has passed away, and he has left you an inheritance with three assets represented symbolically by three coins. Your instructions are that you must share the inheritance fairly, but you cannot split any of the assets. Now, you must try to find a creative solution that will bring you the maximum possible benefit."

When the Palestinian said he would take two coins and give the Israeli one, everyone laughed and the monk said, "Well, ok, you have the power to do that, but you are sowing the seeds of conflict."

The Israeli said he was thinking of taking one coin and giving the Palestinian two.

"Evidently," the monk guessed, "you feel it's worth the risk of investing in your adversary in this way, and hope to somehow benefit in the future from this."

The boys sat down.

Next, the monk asked two young women (again, one was an Israeli, the other, a Palestinian) to repeat the exercise. It was clear where the monk was going with this, but would the girls get it?

"I would keep one coin and give her two," said the Israeli girl. "On the condition that she donates her second one to a charity, maybe a children's hospital."

"Good," said the monk and asked the Palestinian girl if she agreed.

She said, "I would keep one for myself, and give one to her, and say that we should invest the third one together."

The entire audience stood up and applauded the solution.

Negotiating is not a game, and it is not a war, it is what civilised people do to iron out their differences.

"There is no point," the wise monk said, "in figuring out how to get the other side to sign something they cannot live with. A negotiated settlement today is not the end of the story because there is always the day after, and a good negotiator should be thinking about the day after, and the day after that."

13

MAKE THEM BUY

In the wake of the Covid pandemic, as products and brands change and evolve to meet the new normal, salespeople have to worry about changing customer needs and perceptions. Research findings have shown that around 76% of consumers expect salespeople to understand their needs and expectations. But will that be easy? People do not reveal their needs unless probed deeply. When probed, they resent giving information to salespeople, fearing them and anticipating that something they do not need will be thrust upon them. They expect salespeople to be able to understand their needs without asking too many questions like the cops. It is a struggle for salespeople when buyers do not clearly express their needs.

Buyers nowadays spend a lot of time on the internet researching the products they want to buy. With the overload of information, they often get confused and are unable to decide. In that state of confusion, they start asking their friends for referrals. These opinion leader friends are happy to help, but they confuse buyers further while providing them with more and more information. So, buyers seek an expert who is knowledgeable enough to decipher what they want and what exactly they should buy.

There are too many products and brands and opinions and ratings out there. When customers need to buy something urgently, they prefer to buy something they trust—what they have bought before.

With the world on the edge and the pandemic throwing many challenges in the way of businesses, salespeople need to take a fresh look at their highly interactive and in-person selling model to keep their heads above water.

While following the norm of social distancing, things have become a lot more complex. Salespeople who have been selling the 'traditional way' for decades now need to undergo a transition—go remote. Remote selling is the new normal even as the world wakes up from the Covid-induced pause and starts shopping in earnest again.

Let us observe the changes in the buying habits of today's customers. They have stopped buying products merely to meet their needs or expectations. They buy based on:

Trust

Trust is infused by the brand, product, and the salespeople. People buy trust first, before the product. Their perceptions around a brand are built around their experiences. If my washing machine of a popular brand has not given me any problems before then I would prefer more products of the same brand as I trust this brand.

Trust is a fundamental expectation of customer experience, and findings from Adobe's new Future of Marketing Research Series prove just how important earning trust is for businesses. According to the report, consumers show they trust a brand by:

Making more purchases (71%)

Recommending to friends (61%)

Joining a loyalty programme (41%)

Posting positive reviews or comments on social media (40%)

Brand image

Brand image is what the brand stands for. This is a modern-day trend with customers as they become increasingly aware of the planet's needs. They are willing to pay more or prefer to buy from a brand that is working for the greater good by saving water or causing less pollution or contributing to a social cause.

Check out the case of the popular sportswear brand Nike and the steps it is taking to build its image. Nike recently put out a statement saying that it has always believed in the power of sports to make the world a better place. In June 2021, it extended this vision by refurbishing Shek Lei Grind court, a community basketball court in Hong Kong. The court's surface has been created by recycling 20,000 pairs of sneakers. Moreover, the court is in a residential neighbourhood and was chosen for its proximity to 14 schools keeping in mind the region's need for open-air recreational space for children.

To make things more interesting, British artist James Jarvis painted cartoon characters playing basketball there. These appeared across the court and made the area more fun and livelier.

More and more brands today are stating what they stand for and people are buying into the stories they create. Around 75% of young consumers believe that businesses should take greater responsibility and do more to create a better and fairer world for everyone. Brands are remodelling their image stories accordingly.

New-age consumers expect brands to be consistent about the issues they campaign for and will hold them accountable if they fail. Conversely, brands that campaign on an issue that really matters and create a difference in the world will be rewarded with loyalty.

Further, since the onset of Covid-19, consumers have adopted a more cautious, risk-averse attitude to safety, health, and hygiene—another set of standards that call for brands and salespeople to be watchful while making their sales pitches.

Brand culture

Culture, as the late Sumantra Ghoshal said, is the "smell of the place". A brand's culture is experienced by the customer's interactions with the brand. Customers watch carefully what is said, how the people representing the brand treat them, and respond to their requests. The people behind the brand reflect the brand's culture. What they say and do become important for the customer and they carry this as the brand's culture impression. This forms the basis for making buying decisions.

Convenience

The internet has made buying quite convenient. Ease of shopping, hygiene factors, the plethora of options have made it convenient for people to buy online. Driving to a place just to pick up stuff you have bought before or know very well is passé. The omni-retail route is the new way. Earlier, many products needed to be carried around and demonstrated by salespeople. Customers also visited stores to check out what they wanted to buy and stores needed to stock a lot of goods and keep the full line on display. Today, most retail stores stock only new products to demonstrate them and for customers to experience them. The orders are then placed by the customers online (at the store, assisted by the sales staff) and products are shipped to their homes from a central warehouse.

Flaunt value

Flaunt buyers may not desperately need products. They want something new all the time to maintain their image. The point is to say, "I got this new iPhone/camera/laptop, do you have one?" Social media pressure has made such customers buy and choose products and services differently. Conventional selling approaches are not going to work with them. A new way of storytelling needs to be established between the buyer and the seller.

Mood elevation

There is an over-used term for why people shop and seek happiness—retail therapy. It is true though that for some, it is a stress buster just to buy stuff. Buying is a mood elevator. A recent study found that 62% of shoppers across the world buy something to cheer themselves up. So, while selling, salespeople need to be skilled and perceptive enough to discern what and why customers are buying and then work on convincing them to make buying decisions.

The new way of selling will throw up more challenges. It is simple to understand what somebody wants, but will it be easy to understand why somebody is buying and change your sales pitch accordingly? Gone are the days when merely a sales pitch would do to woo customers and make them decide what to buy. It will become more difficult to meet customers to make a pitch effectively in the coming days. Travel costs and cost of selling will soar notwithstanding the need for making products affordable for people to buy them in large volumes to keep manufacturing costs reasonable.

Will it be possible to make multiple visits to customers like before? No. Hence, customer contact will be made mostly through phone calls or video calls. Understanding customer needs and queries through calls, chats, and video meets will be more challenging than meeting them face to face. Imagine showing a variety of products and making a correct pitch in an environment like that. Salespeople will not be able to perform the simple process of greeting, understanding needs, presentation, handling objections, and closing effectively. They may need to adapt and execute their moves like a cricketer or a tennis player. They must anticipate what is coming their way and find the best response skill to effectively handle the situation in front of them.

For example, if you get a call where you need to build trust, you need to use your skills for building rapport. If customers are confused and have many queries, you need to connect and use your understanding skills. If customers need to be persuaded, you need to handle their concerns, persuade, and close. When customers call in a state of distress, you need to use your LEAP-empathy skills.

All the skills highlighted in this book help to establish rapport and connect with the customer; develop a deep understanding of their buying needs; present the value of the product and service; persuade; and ultimately win the customer's trust to come back and buy.

Selling is not a process. It is a skill. It needs to be practised and mastered by first understanding the nuances that are discussed in detail in this book. It is quite akin to learning other skills like singing, dancing, or playing a sport. There is a basic science around which a skill is developed. Practise it till you become perfect and it becomes an art...your art. It stays with you for good then.

I have watched many successful salespeople selling. They have their own styles, which they have honed and mastered. No selling style is a bad one if you successfully acquire a customer and build trust. However, for those who need a specific approach to hone and develop their skills, I hope the techniques explained in this book will help them to master this art.

Robert Louis Stevenson said, "Everyone lives by selling something."

Happy selling to all of you!

Acknowledgements

I wish to show my appreciation to the following people without whom this would not have been possible.

My wife Gayathri who proofed the first draft of the manuscript and shared her invaluable inputs that helped me polish it further. I wish to extend my special thanks to Suhail and his team at The Book Bakers, who found merit in what I wrote and helped to connect me with the right publishing house, Om Books International. I would like to thank its Chief Editor Shantanu Ray Chaudhuri, and my editors Vineetha Mokkil and Jyotsna Mehta for ensuring what I had conceived is understood by anyone with a keen interest in this subject.

Finally, I would like to extend my special thanks to all my customers I met over the last 40 odd years, who have helped me hone my selling skills and have inspired me to share the practical tips with the world at large.